KINGDOM KEYS FOR SUCCESS

PURSUE YOUR DREAM, NO MATTER WHO YOU ARE AND WHERE YOU ARE

Kingstone P. Ngwira

authorHOUSE

AuthorHouse™
1663 Liberty Drive
Bloomington, IN 47403
www.authorhouse.com
Phone: 833-262-8899

Published by AuthorHouse 09/22/2020

ISBN: 978-1-6655-0130-9 (sc)
ISBN: 978-1-6655-0128-6 (hc)
ISBN: 978-1-6655-0129-3 (e)

Library of Congress Control Number: 2020918631

Print information available on the last page.

This book is printed on acid-free paper.

Scripture quotations taken from the Holy Bible, King James Version (Authorized Version). First published in 1611. Quoted from the KJV Classic Reference Bible, Copyright © 1983 by The Zondervan Corporation.

Contents

Dedication

To the God of our Lord Jesus Christ, the Father of Glory who has made us Kings and Priests to reign on the earth.

To all that believe in the King of Kings who has given us the Spirit of Wisdom and the Eyes of Understanding as well as Revelation in the Knowledge of Him.

To all my Pastors, the Eldership and Church Staff of Pentecostal Life Church International (PLCI). Your support, dedication and commitment are truly exceptional.

Acknowledgements

I am excited to point out that this book has taken four (4) years to prepare and two (2) years to write. Many people from different backgrounds encouraged me during both the preparatory and writing time. Indeed there were times when it seemed as if I would never succeed. I am happy to acknowledgee veryone who gave me support, without which, this project could never have been completed.

I wish to thank my wife, Shannila and our children, Pastor Prince and Gift for their patience and understanding during my busy schedules and late-night writing. I am grateful.

Lastly, but by no means least, I would like to thank all staff members at Great Dominion Holdings Limited (GDHL) for their untiring efforts. Your support to make this edition a success is acknowledged with gratitude.

Preface

If you dedicate yourself to applying the Kingdom Keys presented in this book, your dream and vision shall be pursued and attained timely in your life and if you make this book part of your life it will help you succeed in every situation. I can make those statements with complete confidence because the book has success principles that are tested and proven to be life changing.

Early in my real-life ministry, it became obvious to me that revelatory knowledge gives you a big edge in matters of daily life and destiny. When you learn everything about what you are getting into, risk is substantially reduced. People who understand the revelation knowledge—by that I mean savvy and prepared not just formally educated—have the advantage. That is what has made me so successful.

Understanding the Keys of the Kingdom is experiencing incredible rates of growth, not only for ministers of the gospel but also across the world as well. Since the purpose of Keys of the Kingdom is to loosen and bind anything on earth or in heaven, it goes without saying that learning the Keys of the Kingdom will give you success over circumstances of life no matter who you are and where you are.

The purpose of this book is exciting for all that believe in the King of Kings, who has given us the Spirit of Wisdom and the Eyes of understanding. He has also given us the Spirit of Revelation in the Knowledge of Him. To the God of our Lord Jesus Christ, the Father of Glory who has made us Kings and Priests to reign on the earth. I want this book to help everyone who wants to succeed in life. In true sense, no one desires poverty, failure, lack, sickness, mediocrity, stagnation or any form of negativity.

Everyone wants to succeed. No one finds it joyful when a landlord vacates him or her from a rented house. It is not joyful when one's children have been chased from school for failure to pay school fees or because yesterday they slept on an empty stomach.

Success is a journey. Success is not comparing with what others have done but constantly assessing on what you have done or achieved in your strategic vision. That is why I invited the contributors to work on this book with me. Here is a tip for getting the most out of this book. Do not get overwhelmed by all the good ideas and details within this highly resourceful book. Focus on how you can implement the Keys in the next 180 days. If you do, I guarantee, it will put you on the path to success and prosperity, just like the subtitle says.

Most people never take the time to come up with even a basic plan for building their destiny—so by learning from this book, you will improve on your quality of life and people including your enemies will start envying you and will soon go into hiding. So, I encourage you to read this book, but more importantly work on implementation of the Keys!

Kingstone P. Ngwira

Introduction

Thank you for making a decision to read this book. In the pages ahead you are going to learn the Kingdom Keys that will give you **authority** *(Greek, Exousia – the right to do as one is pleased)* and **power***(Greek, Dunamis – might, ability to do)*over circumstances of life. The principles and concepts presented in this book will never leave you the same. You are moving from glory to glory and beginning to change levels in every area of life. Your enemies will look at you three times to confirm if it is really you.

Jesus Christ told Simon Peter, *"And I will give thee keys of the kingdom of heaven: and whatsoever thou shalt bind on earth shall be bound in heaven: and whatsoever thou shalt loose on earth shall be loosed in heaven"*, *(*Matthew 16:19).

Keys of the Kingdom of God are designed to answer questions like: Who am I? - Identity; Where am I from? - Source; Why am I here? – Purpose; What Can I do? – Potential; and Where am I going? – Destiny. The Keys will give you authority and power to reign over the earth in general and to reign in your specific assignment in a particular domain. *The word key as used in Matthew 16:19 uses the Greek word 'Kleis'. It means, an ability to open the doors of faith, while also functioning on earth, as expected in heaven by Christ.*

I have discovered that the original plan of God was to extend the kingdom of God to the earth. Kingdom Keys are there for you so that you have accessa to the realm that makes you enjoy God's Kingdom while on the earth, as Jesus prayed ... *Your Kingdom come, Your WILL be done on the earth as it is in heaven ...* You begin to move in the Kingdom dimension and in God's WILL by using the Keys of the Kingdom.

"And I appoint unto you a kingdom, as my father hath appointed unto me", **Luke 22:29.** God wants you to rule over the earth.......

The value of the Keys of the Kingdom is either maximized or minimized by our perception. ***Perception determines reception.*** We can only enjoy life to the degree that we know and maximize the Keys of the Kingdom. They are a source of our supplies. Paul says, ***"But my God shall supply all your needs according to His riches in glory by Christ Jesus", (Philippians 4:19).***

Sometime ago through my own observation as well as reading literature widely, I discovered that the greatest threat to one's future is religion. Religion can be so powerful and controlling to a person. It can be so powerful than politics, military arms as well as scientific advancement? Because religion is not just a social, cultural, political or ideological factor; instead it finds its influence in the personal chambers of one's soul. Within the souls, we discover the source of the private motivation that forms perceptions and behavior. Man is more willing to die for the sake of his religion than for any political, social, or ideological reason. This is why Jesus's coming to the earth was not to establish a religion but a Kingdom of God which operates on keys. The kingdom of God must influence you, not religion

This book will enhance your passion to understand the Keys of the Kingdom of God. It will help you to take charge over the circumstances of life and your destiny. You will also be able to live your life to the fullest, as you reconnect your life to your true identity and authority.

"You shall know the truth and the truth shall make you free" (**John 8:32**).

It is now time to search for the ideal truth. You may wish to know that the driving force and desire for the perfect world finds its way into every civilization and has been the source of inspiration that has led to the invention of philosophical ideas, social infrastructures and even religion. This force is centralized in man's search for the ideal. The Kingdom Keys are the ideal aspect that must be searched. And in this book, you will discover them.

So we can identify what we lack by what we naturally desire and thus recognize our need which is to learn the Kingdom Keys that will help us to overcome the circumstances of life no matter who we are and where we are. We will discuss this need in the succeeding chapters.

Welcome on board!!

Part I

THE NATURE OF THE KINGDOM

CHAPTER 1

The King of Kings and the Kingdom

Let me start by saying, I wish I knew then what I know now. This is also one of the lamenting songs of many men and women of God. However, it is not too late for a glorious shift. *"In the beginning God created the heavens and the earth", Genesis 1:1.* This verse refers to two Kingdoms: the Kingdom of God and the Earthly Kingdom. It goes without saying that the Kingdom of God is an invisible realm where we have the invisible God. *"Now unto the King eternal, immortal, invisible, the only wise God, be honour and glory forever and ever. Amen."* (1 **Timothy 1:17**). This means that God is King of Kings and is the creator of the two Kingdoms, Heaven and Earth. According to Genesis 2:15, God took the man, and put him into the Garden of Eden to dress and to keep it. This is the introduction of the earthly Kingdom. Adam was given the earthly Kingdom to rule, to govern or to manage. However, though we have two Kingdoms in existence God is the creator of the two Kingdoms.

The question that comes to mind is "What is a Kingdom?" A kingdom is about a King and his Children. A Kingdom is about a King and his domain. A kingdom is about a King and a Royal Family. Therefore, the message of the Bible is about a King, a Kingdom and His royal offspring.

1 Peter 2:9 says *"But ye are a chosen generation, a royal priesthood, a holy nation, a peculiar people, that ye should shew forth the praises of Him who hath called you out of darkness into His marvelous light".*

So, in pursuit of understanding our roles as Kings, we need to appreciate the birth of Jesus who was announced at His birth as a King. This is very important because it emphasizes the primary focus of the mission of Jesus and His purpose for coming to the earth. Luke presents this statement, *"The law and the prophets were until John: since that time the Kingdom of God is preached and every man presseth into it"* (Luke 16:16)).

Every one of the 7 billion people on planet Earth is seeking the Kingdom of God, which is their ultimate fulfillment. This is why every religion and activity of mankind is man's attempt to find or discover the Kingdom. Therefore, it is necessary that we all understand the nature of the Kingdoms so that we can all appreciate the good news brought to earth by our Lord Jesus Christ.

The purpose for the coming of Jesus to the earth is clear. But He said, *"I must preach the good news of the kingdom of God to other towns also, because that is why I was sent"*(Luke 4:43). Many bible scholars say that purpose is the original entity or motivation for something. Purpose can also be defined as the reason or desired result for the initiation or an action of production of something. Purpose determines what is right. Purpose has a role of protecting us from doing something wrong at the expense of the right. This means that purpose is a function of ethics. People all over the world are in dilemma whether to do right things or wrong things. In some instances, people would want to do the wrong thing and think that it is the right thing to do.

It is really interesting to observe that the promise of the inheritance is of the earth rather than heaven. Genesis 1:28 says, *"And God blessed them, and God said unto them, 'Be fruitful, and multiply, and replenish the earth, and subdue it: and subdue it and have dominion over the fish of the sea and over the fowl of the air, and over every living thing that moveth upon the earth'.*The scripture suggests that man's purpose is to have dominion over the earth. John the revelator in Revelation 5:10 concurs with this thinking when he eschatologically says, *"And has made us unto our God kings and priests: and we shall reign on the earth"*.

When Adam lost the kingdom to Satan, he lost this dominion. So too if any man loses the kingdom he or she loses his or her dominion. It is important to know that the message of the Kingdom of God because it is the most important news ever delivered to the human race. Jesus came to earth to announce the arrival of the Kingdom and to establish it in the hearts of people through His death and His resurrection. As evidenced in the scriptures to all those who believed in Him, Jesus restored their citizenship rights in the Kingdom of God so that they could represent Him and the government of heaven on earth. Many biblical commentators say that this representation is called government diplomacy.

All true Kingdoms have similar characteristics. They all embrace the Kingdom Principles of Kings: Kingdom Lordship Principle; Domain Principle; Constitution Principle; Law Principle; Kingdom Keys Principle, Citizenship Principle; Commonwealth Principle; Culture Principle; Economy Principle; Taxation Principle; Army Principle; Delegated Authority Principle; Ambassador Principle; Education Principle; Administration Principle; Principle of Glory; Principle of Worship; Principle of Provision; Principle of Influence; Principle of Decree and Principle of Giving among others.

The following scripture could be perceived as a political statement that is very common to all kingdoms.

"And I confer on you a kingdom, just as my Father conferred one on Me" **(Luke 22:29).**

This statement has been adopted at the appointment of an official representative of a government to other nations. This is called, the position of an ambassador. Every nation appoints ambassadors to represent its interests to other nations. The Kingdom of God is no different. God chooses to communicate the message of His Kingdom on the earth through personal representatives. This is God's chosen strategy. An ambassador is a political appointee whose job is to represent and speak for his or her home government before the rulers of other countries.

Good ambassadors never speak their personal opinions but only the official policies of the government that appointed them. In the same way, the people of God are His ambassadors on the earth. **"We are therefore Christ's ambassadors, as though God were making His appeal through us. We implore you on Christ's behalf: Be reconciled to God." (Corinthians 5:20).** It is important to know that as God's ambassadors, we represent our Father's Kingdom on earth.

CHAPTER 2

God's Original Plan

God's original plan is what I would call God's Great Idea. God's idea was that He extends the Kingdom of God to the earth. It was God's idea to share His invisible Kingdom with His off springs, which He called mankind and give them His nature and characteristics. This means that God who is an invisible God (1 Timothy 1:17), who is in invisible realm, created the heavens and the earth (Genesis 1:1). God did this because He wanted to rule the visible earth from the invisible heaven through His spiritual children created in heaven and deployed to the visible earth. *So, God's original plan is to rule the earth through human presentation.*

It was God's desire to create sons in His image. *Genesis 1:26, says: "And God said let us create man in our own image, after our likeness: and let them have dominion over the fish of the sea, and over the fowl of the air, and over the cattle and over all the earth and over every creeping thing that creepeth upon the earth."* Based on this scripture, it is clear that we are all created in God's image after His likeness. This is a call for every one reading this book, to begin to represent God and the Kingdom of God here on earth as an ambassador.

"Now then we are ambassadors for Christ, reconciling the world unto himself, not imputing their trespasses unto them and hath committed unto us the word of reconciliation."(1 Corinthians 5:20)

It goes without saying that it is not good to ask God, the King of Kings, the King of heaven, why He created the heavens and the earth. And He wanted to rule the earth from heaven through children created in His image. May be the question that comes to your mind is,'Was God not satisfied with an invisible realm of angels to rule?' The answer to such a question is to understand the nature of the almighty God Himself. In my view there is just too much to know and understand about the very nature of God Himself who has already revealed Himself to us so that we all understand His character.

From the above presentation a conclusion can be made that man was created to exercise power and designated to manage it. Genesis 1:28 says, *"And God blessed them, and God said unto them, be fruitful and multiply and replenish the earth and subdue it and have dominion over the fish of the sea and over the fowl of the air and over every living thing that moveth upon the earth."* This scripture shows that the motivating factor for the creation of human kind was to dominate the earth and its resources, the result of the Creator's desire to extend His ruler ship from the invisible heaven to the visible earth.

To be given dominion means to be established as a sovereign, king ruler, master, governor, responsible for reigning over a designated territory, with the inherent authority to represent and embody as a symbol, the territory, resources and all that constitutes the kingdom. This statement must be understood by every man with a view to understand the original purpose, will and plan of God our Creator, the King of Kings.

God's plan and program was to implement His own idea of extending the kingdom of God to the earth and to rule the visible earth from the invisible supernatural realm through a family of spiritual children. *"But as many as received Him, to them gave ye power to become the sons of God, even to them that believe on his name.", John 1:12.* This is why the disturbed order of the Kingdom of God on earth through the first Adam was considered rebellion against the eternal imperial Kingdom of Heaven and the creating of a vagabond state. The fall of Adam was not the fall of man from heaven but fall of man from the earth. It is important to understand that Adam did not lose heaven when he fell; rather he lost legal representation of heaven on earth. His fall made the earth a territory under illegal government.

We thank God for the second Adam who came to restore back the lost kingdom back to man. He came to restore back the lost ruler ship, glory, dominion, power and authority back to man.

"And so, it is written, the first Adam was made a living soul; that last Adam was made a quickening spirit" (1 Corinthians 15:45).

The fall of man in the Garden of Eden resulted into a promise. Genesis 3:15-16, says, ***"And I will put enemity between you and the woman, and between your offspring and hers; He will crush your head, and you will strike his heel."*** To the woman He said, "I will greatly increase your pains in childbearing; with pain you will give birth to children. Your desire will be for your husband and he will rule over you." The heart and soul of the above promise is the coming of an "offspring" through a woman who would break the power of the enemy over mankind and regain the authority and dominion Adam once held and through the process restore the Kingdom back to mankind. This promise gave hope for the entire Kingdom which was lost to Satan. This means that the greatest need of man today is to find out what he had earlier lost, which is the Kingdom.

The God's restoration programme is therefore the establishment of His Kingdom on the visible earth. This therefore would be seen as the ultimate reason or purpose of the promised Messiah. The following are the consequences which came as a function of rebellion: loss of position and disposition; fear; loss of power and authority; transfer of responsibility; loss of domination over nature; frustrated toil and hatred of labour; pain and discomfort; the need for human accountability and self - consciousness and shame.

It is on this premise that God launched a journey and had set and followed a path to find us. This means that our God, the King of Kings is the chaser and we are the pursued. God, the Father who dwells in heaven, came down to take hold of us. His purpose was to restore back the kingdom to us. This is what I call Kingdom restoration. The restoration of God's Kingdom and ruler ship on earth through mankind is truly what lies at the heart of our faith.

It is for this reason that we can say it joyfully that the Kingdom of God has come on earth. Jesus's message, which was given to Him by His father, reflected His divine mission on earth as well as the passion and desire of His heart. Here is the first statement Jesus said when He came to earth and started His ministry, "From that time Jesus began to preach, and to say, 'Repent for the Kingdom of Heaven is at hand.' Jesus came to preach the message of the Kingdom. Luke concurs with this statement when he presents the same thinking in ***Luke 4:43, "And he said unto them, I must*** *preach the Kingdom of God to other cities also: for therefore am sent."* As an extension to the *John18;37 says, "… Jesus answered, thou sayest that I am a King. To this end was I was born and for this cause came I into the world that I should bear witness unto the truth…"*

CHAPTER 3

The Culture of the Kingdom of God

The Kingdom of God is about a King who is eternal, immortal, invisible, the only wise God and His children whom He calls sons. The Kingdom of God is about a royal family. The bible says in *1 Peter 2:9, (But ye are the chosen generation, a royal priest hood, a holy nation, a peculiar people, that ye should shew forth the praises of him who hath called you out of darkness to His marvelous light."* The Kingdom of God is life itself. The origin of the Kingdom of God is traced from *Genesis 1:1, which says, "In the beginning God created the heaven and the earth." God created the heaven and called it Kingdom of Heaven.*

From what has been presented above, it is important and necessary that we all understand the concepts and principles of Kingdoms so that we appreciate the good news brought to the earth by Jesus the Christ. Let me point out that all Kingdoms have a culture. Here are the concepts and principles of the culture of the kingdom of God that you should understand.

The Kingdom of heaven is about the principle of Kings. The King who is God Himself is the essence of His kingdom. The king is the ultimate source of authority and through His authority, He established the kingdom of God. This means that the sovereignty of the King is reflected in His royal authority. *In this case the word of a King in the kingdom becomes law.* ThisKing of the kingdom is never voted into power and cannot be voted out of power. He is from everlasting to everlasting. He chooses who will be a citizen in His kingdom (1 Peter 2:19). The presence of a king is the presence of his entire kingdom authority. And Jesus is that King.

"You are a king, then!" said Pilate. Jesus answered, "You are right in saying I am a king. In fact, for this reason I was born, and for this I came unto the world, to testify to the truth, everyone on the side of truth listens to Me" (John 18:37).

They will make war against the Lamb, but the Lamb will overcome them because He is Lord of lords and King of Kings and with Him will be His called, chosen and faithful followers (Revelation 17:14. The kingdom of heaven recognizes the lordship principle. It goes without saying that all true kings must have property or dominion over which they exercise ruler ship of dominion. This means that all true kings are personally legal owners of property, territory or their domain. The word owner also means "lord."

All true Kings therefore are automatically lords. This is why Jesus is called "Lord of Lord," We are lords over our domain or territories here on earth. So, this implies that we are lords here on earth. The principle of lordship says that kings have absolute authority and control over their property. The King's wealth is measured by the wealth of his property. This is why kings can give their property to anyone they wish.

No wonder Paul sees God Almighty as the supplier.*"But my God shall supply all your needs according to His riches in glory by Christ Jesus"* (Philippians 4:19).

"The silver is mine, and the gold is mine, saith the LORD of hosts", Haggai 2:9.

The earth is the Lord's and everything in it, the world, and all who live in it: for He founded it upon the sea and established it upon the waters, Psalm 24:1-2.

How awesome is the Lord Most High, the great King over all the earth! Psalm 47:2.

That if you confess with your mouth, "Jesus is Lord," and believe in your heart that God raised Him from the dead, you will be saved, Romans 10:9.

The second principle of the kingdom of God is the domain principle. The domain of a King is the territory over which he exercises authority, control and dominion. The King owns his domain and expand or extend it by the power of His might, that is why in previous chapters, I talked about the original plan of God to extend His kingdom, to the earth. This shows that Kingdoms expand by colonizing territories. When Adam lost the Kingdom to Satan Jesus was sent to the earth to colonize the earth.

From the above statement it shows that Adam lost the kingdom to Satan because he wanted to become independent. ***Independence is not equal to freedom. So too deliverance is not equal to freedom. I have seen many people that are delivered but they are not free.*** *"And ye shall know the truth and the truth shall make you free"* (**John 8:32**).

The wealth of the domain determines the King's glory. When the King impacts the domain with his influence, it is called his "kingdom." This sees the King delegating authority to others to share in the governing and administration of his domain.

"His domain is an eternal dominion; His kingdom endures from generation to generation. All the peoples of the earth are regarded as nothing. He does as He pleases with the powers of heaven and the peoples of the earth. No one can hold back His hand or say to Him, what have you done?", ***Daniel 4:34-35.***

From the above scripture it shows that God, the King of Kings and Lord of Lords, His domain is the kingdom of God but He wants to extend His rulership to the earth through human representation. The domain for man is the earth but God is the Lord of Lords and King of Kings. ***"The earth is the LORD's and the fullness therefore; the world, and they that dwell therein"*** (**Psalm 24:1**).

In this chapter I cannot leave out the Kingdom Citizenship Principle. From my presentation in this book it is clear that when we become born again we automatically enter into the Kingdom of God and become citizens of heaven and it is from this truth that Paul calls us Ambassadors for Christ (2 Corinthians 5:20). Remember that though you are in the world you are not of the world. This means that there is one earth but two worlds. These different worlds are called Kingdom of God or Kingdom of the Light and Kingdom of Satan or Kingdom of Darkness. The world in which you are depends on who rules over you.

But He contained, ***"You are from below; I am from above. You are of this world; I am not of this world"***, **John 8:23.**

On my study on the message of the Kingdom, I have concluded that citizenship in the kingdom is not a right but a privilege because we are chosen by Grace. Not that there is anything we have done right. Citizens are chosen by a King and are beneficiaries of the King's pleasure and promises. But our citizenship is in heaven, and we eagerly await a Saviour from there, the Lord Jesus Christ, who by the power that enables Him to bring everything under His control, will transform our lowly bodies so that they will be like His glorious body (Philippians 3:20-21).

Jesus said, *"my kingdom is not of this world. If it were, my servants would fight to prevent My arrest by the Jews. But now My kingdom is from another place"* (John 18:36).

The other concept of the kingdom of God is the Kingdom principle of keys. The keys of the Kingdom are the principles, laws and systems by which the Kingdom functions. Therefore, this is a call that the keys must be learned and understood and applied by the citizens in order to appropriate the benefits and privileges of the Kingdom.

***"I will give you the keys of the kingdom of heaven; whatever you bind on earth will be bound in heaven and whatever you loose on earth will be loosed in heaven"* (Mathew 16:19).**

This leads us to the principle of common wealth. All kingdoms function on the principal of a common wealth. Common wealth is the King's commitment to see that all of his citizens have equal access to the wealth and resources of the kingdom. Many people say that the quality of life of the citizens in the Kingdom reflects the glory and reputation of the king. This means that when the welfare of the King's citizens is excellent, then the king's reputation among other kings is honorable. Kingdoms provides for the needs of their citizens and the king is personally committed to and involved in the welfare of his citizens.

***So do not worry, saying "What shall we eat?" or "What shall we drink?" "What shall we wear?" For the pagans run after all these things and your heavenly father knows that you need them, But seek ye first the kingdom and His righteousness and all these things will be given to you as well*(Mathew 6:31-33).**

CHAPTER 4

The Government of the Kingdom of Heaven versus the Government of Man

Many Theological and Social commentators, as well as Church leaders, are attaching all the national and international problems faced in our world today, to either governmental or religious crisis. They say that, this includes global hunger, health epidemics and pandemics, wars, terrorism, racial and ethnic conflicts, segregation, nuclear tension, and economic uncertainty. Throughout history, man's greatest challenge has been to learn how-to live-in peace with himself and his neighbors. Dr. Myles Munroe in his book: Kingdom Principles mentions that whether it is the continent of Africa, Old Europe, Norsemen of England, the Mongols of Asia, Indians of North and South America, or the Eskimos of Iceland, tribal warfare, racial and ethnic conflicts, and full-scale war have been the human story. He says in all of these social and cultural expressions of humanity, the one thing that has always evolved was some kind of authority structure, a form of leadership or government mechanism to establish and maintain social order. Government type decides destiny type. *The Greek word for Government is 'Kubernesis', it means steering or pilotage. A car will not get to its destination because of speed but direction. That steering to destination is called Government.*

It goes without saying that the need for governmentand order is inherent in the human spirit and is a manifestation of adivine mandate given to mankind by the Creator. Man was created to be a governor and ruler, and therefore, it is his nature to seek some authority mechanism that would bring order to his private and social world. Government is necessary, desirable, and essential to man's social context no matter how primitive or modern. This is why man continues to search for an effective way to govern himself. Man's need for some formal government structure is an out-growth of his need for social order and relationship management. This need begins in the smallest prototype of society, the family and extends all the way to the manifestation of national expressions of constitutional order.

Nations need government. The first Book of Moses, Genesis, reveals that the first prototype of governance was introduced by the Creator Himself long before. Adam and Eve existed on the earth. In fact, it gives evidence of a government structure that preexisted earth and the physical universe itself. This expression of government structure was a result of a desire to bring order to chaos and productivity to emptiness. ***Now the earth was formless [no order]and empty [chaotic emptiness], darkness was over the surface of the deep, and the Spirit of God was hovering over the waters. And God said, 'Let there be light', Genesis 1:2-3.*** Here we see that the impact of a divine, invisible, supernatural government was necessary because of disorder and chaos. Thus, the purpose for government is to maintain order and manage productivity. Furthermore, the creation of mankind was also a result of disorder and the need for management. A little later in Genesis, we find evidence of this as one of God's motives for creating man. When the Lord God made the earth and the heavens—and no shrub of the field had yet appeared on the earthly Kingdom because there was no man to govern the Domain.

Man has been attempting to establish a form of self-government that would alleviate the internal and external chaos he continues to experience. But there is no such governance unless he functions within his delegated ambassadorial position. Anytime man shuns his dominion calling on the earth, there is chaos manifested even in the physical creation he was mandated to govern—the earth.

This is the reality behind the statement of the first-century biblical writer, Paul, when he wrote: ***The creation waits in eager expectation for the sons of God to be revealed. For the creation was subjected to frustration, not by its own choice, but by the will of the one who subjected it, in hope that the creation itself will be liberated from its bondage to decay and brought into the glorious freedom of the children of God (Romans 8:19-21).*** Paul's statement reveals the fact that government affects not only the people of the land but also the land and its physical environment.

Based on the presentation above, it clearly shows that governance is serious business. When man rejected heavenly ordained governance, he became the source of his own governing program. The results ever since have proven our intensive need for help. The Creator's intent was to administrate the earthly government from Heaven through His created image (Imago Dei) in man and thus manifest His nature and character on earth. God's government is a unique structure that is still misunderstood. I would at this point describe it as a corporate Kingdom government. Government by corporate leadership! ***The kingdom of God is a theocratic order of a King over kings as partners in governing!*** This is what we would call the "Kingdom of God." The kingdom government concept is God's idea. However, when man rejected heaven's government, he had no choice but to accept as an alternative the disappointing plethora of human attempts to govern.

When the children of Israel left the land of Egypt, as recorded in the book of Exodus, God instructed Moses to advise them that they would be governed by the laws of heaven and led by God Himself as their heavenly King on the earth. This was the first step in God's plan to reinstate the Kingdom of God on earth, using a small nation of freed slaves as His prototype. He expressed His divine desire through Moses, stating: ***"Now if you obey Me fully and keep My covenant, then out of all nations you will be My treasured possession. Although the whole earth is mine, you will be for Me a Kingdom of priests and a holy nation." These are the words you are to speak to the Israelites,*** **(Exodus 19:5-6).** God's intention for the earth is that it should be governed by heaven and from heaven. Israel rejected theocracy, the rule of a gracious and loving King who would protect and provide for them. Instead, they substituted a divine King for a human king. Their decision led to calamitous consequences.

The fall of man was not the loss of heaven but rather the loss of the Kingdom government of heaven on earth. Any honest human taking a serious look at the conditions of our planet would have to conclude that earth needs a new, or in this case, an alternative form of government. The spiritual, social, economic, physical, environmental, and cultural conditions of our earth demand a government that is superior to any we have yet invented. Perhaps the answer to man's need for an effective and just government is found in the first official words of Jesus Christ two thousand years ago as He announced His primary mission and commented on the human condition: From that time on, Jesus began to preach, ***"Repent, for the kingdom of heaven is near"*** **(Matthew 4:17).**

Blessed are the poor in spirit, for theirs is the Kingdom of heaven (Matthew 5:3). Here we note that Jesus' assessment of man's spiritual and social hunger and poverty of soul can be satisfied only by receiving the Kingdom of God. The Kingdom is the only source of true joy, peace and righteousness, Romans 14:17. Jesus' announcement that the kingdom of God is near, identified His stated solution to man's earthly condition: The Kingdom concept originated in the mind of God and was the original governing system designed for earth. The ideal Kingdom concept is unique, distinctive, and provides for the greatest benefits to its citizens. The ideal Kingdom is such a beautiful idea that only God could have thought of it. And it is the only system of governing ghat can bring the peace, equality, and fulfillment that mankind longs for.

I use the term "ideal Kingdom" concept because historically man has attempted to imitate and duplicate the heavenly design of the Kingdom with disappointing results. Man's efforts to establish his own government has produced defective, oppressive, and destructive models that have not only fallen short of the noble aspirations of man but has also inflicted negative repercussions on his fellow man. In essence, mankind's rejection of God's Kingdom model has led to the abolition of peace and the installation of inferior forms of government. Some governments are better than others, but all are inferior to God's government—the Kingdom of God.

The Government of Man versus the Government of Heaven

The Bible is the most misunderstood book on planet earth, not only by those who do not prescribe to it, but also by many of those who claim to know and embrace its message. Simply stated, the Bible is about a King, a Kingdom, and a royal family of children. The Bible is not about religion and was never intended to be a religious book. Rather, its story and message are about the desire of a King to extend His Kingdom to new territories through His royal family. The Bible, therefore, is about government and governing.

What is government? ***Government is about order, influence, administration, distribution, protection, maintenance, accountability, responsibility and productivity.*** Technically speaking, government isa Kingdom person, group, or organization that executes the functions of governing. This is manifested in the exercise of authority and jurisdiction over territory and a citizenry. Government was first established by the command and mandate of God to Adam and incorporates the need to order, work, oversee, guard, and protect.

The roots of government in the western world reach back to theworld of the Greeks. In Greek, government (kubernites) literally means to steer, to pilot, or to act as a rudder. Without the government and its Law, we have chaos. So, government is the power given or derived for the purpose of making and enforcing laws for a certain territory. Governing incorporates the concepts of both power and authority. These two are distinct from each other and must be fully under-stood in order to appreciate the proper context of government.

Both authority and power must be in balance for government to be successful. Authority has to do with responsibility while power has to do with ability. Authority has to do with empowerment; power focuses on exercising authority. Authority gives power its legality. Power without legitimate authority is dictatorship and inevitably results in abuse, oppression, and destruction. Authority gives power and its rights. Authority is the key to successful government. If the ruling power does not have authority, it cannot govern. The authority to govern either is given by way of a popular vote or derived by way of inherent authority.

Earthly governments derive their authority from the people either through a process of choice or by usurping authority by force. For instance, a President or Premier or Prime Minister is imbued with authority by the people who voted him or her into power. In kingdoms, however, authority is inherent and a product of the rights of ownership. This concept is crucial in understanding the nature of kingdoms. God's authority as King is inherent. No one gives Him authority. He has authority because of who He is and the Kingdom of God versus the Government of Man because He created the earth and everything that lives on the earth. That is why Jesus could say that all authority had been given to Him. His Father has all authority and therefore had the right to give it to His Son.

The Father had creative rights to the whole universe. The governments of this earth get their authority by way of vote or violence. It is not inherent authority. The only government on the earth that represents inherent authority is a monarchy. A King has the power and can give it to whomever he chooses. All other governments are formed by casting a vote or by launching a revolution. In the final analysis, all human governments are substitutions for the ideal, no matter how good these governments might be. Let us take a brief look at some of man's attempts at government and structures of ruler ship.

During the early Middle Ages, the economic and social power of societies were related to agriculture; therefore, land was the key source of power. He who owned the land owned the power. When land is power, then whoever owns the most land controls everyone and everything. This is where the idea of "real estate" originated. Landowners were the ones who were considered to possess real estate. The landowner was the "lord" of the land. Thus, we find the word landlord used to describe those who owned land. Therefore, the primary pursuit of all who desired power was land. Landowners were known as lords and eventually became "rulers" of their land. The more land they owned the greater their lordship, or rulership. Individuals who owned significant parcels of land became known as "kings." In other words, the prerequisite for becoming a king was the ownership of land. This is also where the Kingdom Principles idea of earthly kingdoms gets its birth. "Kingdom" was the word used to describe the territory over which a local king, or landowner, ruled or exercised ownership right and authority.

It is also important to note that because all the land was person-ally owned by the landlord, then private property was not possible; thus, all the people who lived on and worked the land did so at the pleasure and mercy of the King or Landlord. Everything in the land, including animals, natural resources, and all other materials, were considered the personal property of the King or lord. In many cases, where the Lord or King was kind and benevolent, the people who lived, worked, and served on his land enjoyed the benefits of his kindness. And because they made his land productive and added prosperity to him, he provided, protected, and cared for them.

This is why a good king tended to attract many to his King-dom.

Feudalism as a concept of governing was a derivative of the original government established in the Garden of Eden under the first man, Adam, who himself was made the landlord of the earth. God's original plan was a feudal system where all men served as Kings and lords of the earth, ruling not humans but the animal, plant, bird, and water Kingdoms. However, in cases where the Landlord or King was not kind and merciful, the result was abuse and oppression of the people by virtue of noble status. Whoever owned the land controlled those who lived on the land.

Feudalism is an illustration of the danger of putting the authority that belongs to the King of heaven into the hands of ungodly and unrighteous human kings and lords. When the culture migrated away from agriculture to industry, the noble lords eventually lost their power.

Dictatorship

Dr. Myles Munroe in his book: Rediscovering the Kingdom, points out that the Government of Man is that individuals are chosen by the gods or by providence to rule them asses and exercise authority over the less fortunate or so called" "inferior" peoples. This is the form of governing we find in the biblical records and other sources such as the Egyptian pharaohs, who believed they were products of the gods and were destined to rule people by virtue of birthright. Dictatorships have emerged in every generation and continue to do so to this day.

They come in many forms and titles, but the principle and results are the same. A dictatorship is government that concentrates its power and authority in the hands of one individual who wields absolute authority unrestricted by laws, constitution, or any other social/political factor. Dictators are considered despots and usually are driven by personal ambition or private interests. They focus in on themselves and their goals. Self-worship is also common in this form of governing.

Historically, dictatorships have never succeeded for long, usually ending in tragedy and chaos. No dictatorship will survive forever. At some point, the people will revolt. The dictatorship is also a twisted attempt by man to reestablish the original form of government established by the Creator in the Garden of Eden when He delegated total rulership and dominion control to the man. Adam was given absolute power, but the distinction was that his power and dominion were never intended to ruleover other human beings but over the animal, bird, plant, and water Kingdoms. Whenever the attempt is made to dominate human kind through any form of dictatorship, the natural result is rebellion and resistance. This is natural and always will be. Dictatorship over humanity is not God's original form of government.

Communism

Dr. Myles Munroe in his book: Rediscovering the Kingdom says as a form of government, communism is a combination of the first two types of governing. He further affirms that communism is man's attempt to control land and people by the exercise of dictatorship. This is why a communist state repossesses all private property and attempts to enforce productivity through oppression and coercion.

It seeks to accomplish this by attempting to legislate loveand sharing, an approach that never succeeds because human nature cannot be forced to love or to care. These behaviors result from natural motivation and internal convictions. No law can accomplish that. It is my view that communism is man's attempt to reestablish the Kingdom of heaven on earth as given to the first man Adam, but without the involvement of the source of creation Himself. In essence, communism is an attempt to establish a kingdom without righteousness. One can find in the writings of Marx and Engels certain sincerity as they sought to find a way to bring power to the people (proletariat) by wresting that power from the hands of then obility (bourgeois).

It was an attempt to take ownership of land away from the nobles and put it in the hands of the people. They believed in a dictatorship of the people. Great idea? Maybe. The only problem is that government is in the hands of people. Whenever man is involved, government will fail. Communism simply exchanged power by wresting it from the hands of the czars and placing it in the hands of a new set of dictators.

Socialism

Many writers say that socialism, is a stepchild of communism, and is another endeavor to bring the state closer to the needs of the people. It substitutes the state for the king and attempts to control society for the benefit of society. Like all the others, socialism is another failed attempt by man to govern himself. Absolute power corrupts absolutely, and the state loses its concern for the individual as it becomes more obsessed with its own power. This leads us to our final look at man's attempt to govern himself.

Democracy

Dr. Myles Munroe in his book: Rediscovering the Kingdom mentions that democracy has its roots in the writings of the Greeks and is viewed by many people (even those in the Western religions) as the perfect government. Plato called it the fairest of constitutions but did so only reluctantly because he saw weaknesses within democracy that would lead to its downfall. The rule of the people, by the people, and for the people is a fine idea. It is man's attempt to get further away from despotism and tyrannical rule. Democracy as a principle is man's reaction to all the other forms of government such as feudalism, dictatorship, communism, and socialism.

A close study of the roots of western democracy will reveal that it was a reaction and rebellion against a divine choice or feudal system of governing called a kingdom. In reality, America was built on rebellion against a Kingdom. The founders and framers of the American concept of governing championed the cause of democracy and adopted the Greek ideas and refined them to accommodate their aspirations. America rejected a kingdom. America's dream and guiding principles were independence, self-determination, and individuality; but while these principles serve as the bedrock of Western democracy, they remain contrary to the Kingdom principles.

Americans have never understood the potential power of a king and his kingdom because they were exposed to corrupt kings. Out of that fear they created a system of rule that would limit the power of a single man. The system of checks and balances was installed to guard against power and authority being consolidated into the hand of one individual. This fear of totalitarianism and dictatorship is the engine that drives the motor of Western democracy, and unstably so. In the absence of the original perfect and ideal Kingdom government concept, the concept of democracy is the best form of government invented by mankind and serves to protect him from his own defective nature and character. However, despite the fact that democracy is the best civil form of governing in our stressful world of demigods, democracy itself is plagued with defects that leave it wanting.

The fundamental problem of democracy is its very foundation, power, and authority by majority vote. Democracy is the best form of civil government as we know it because of its basic tenets and because of the checks and balances of the system. It is also built on the premise and principle of the "majority rule" and the protection of individual rights. Democracy has served our nations well in that it has given voice to the people and provides opportunity for broad-based participation in the political process by the people of a nation. Its checks and balances system further protects the masses from monopolization of power by one or by the few.

Despite its advantages and benefits, however, democracy does come with a few crucial defects. One such defect is its fundamental and major principle of "majority rule." This defect is critical because even though it gives power to the majority of the people, at the same time it places morality, values, and the standards for law at the mercy of the majority vote, thus legitimizing the majority's values, desires, beliefs, aspirations, and preferences. If the power of democracy is in the people, then "we the people" become the sovereign of our lives and corporate destiny, and thus become our own providential ruler and god. This is the reemergence and manifestation of the age-old philosophy of humanism.

Humanism is simply man becoming his own measure for morality, judgment, and justice that places man at the mercy of himself. So, no matter how educated man may become, he can lead himself only as far as he goes himself. The record of history and the present state of the world gives evidence that man left to himself makes a poor god. Therefore, democracy without accountability to one greater than the people is an exercise in moral roulette. Simply put, democracy without God is man's worship and elevation of himself and his own intelligence. What a tragedy!

Democracy cannot succeed without God any more than communism can succeed without God. God is not subject to our politics, nor can He be, but He has created His own political system and governmental structure which, as this book will demonstrate, is far superior to all forms of earthly government. The word politic comes from the Greek word 'politikos', it means the art of governance or leadership. From the Creator's perspective, life is political, and He is the essence of life. In Him there isno distinction between government and spirituality. They are one and the same. The assignment given to the first man in the Garden of Eden was a political assignment given to a spirit being living in afresh body. Therefore, in the context of the original biblical mandate, the concept of the separation of church and state or religion and government is a lofty idea that has no root in biblical logic or fact.

On the other hand, when the majority votes in violation of natural law and of the principles established by the biblical text, that vote or legislation becomes illegitimate. In essence, the problem with democracy—rule of the people—is that the vote of many can be the wrong vote. Another weakness of democracy is that it is not absolute. Its concepts and laws can blow like the wind. It can be easily influenced by the changing culture. Because the citizens can be so easily manipulated by a shift in the culture and by the will of people at the top, they can be induced to abandon their rights and transfer them to those who rule over them.

Plato knew that eventually the rule of the people would deteriorate into the rule of the state. I predict with great sadness that even democracy, with all of its promises and aspirations for a good, civil, and just society, will not survive as a human government. When your best is not good enough, the only alternative is to look else-where for something better. There is a better alternative...and that is the heart of this book.

Part II

AFTER THE FALL OF MAN

Chapter 5

Reasons for Jesus's coming to the Earth

Based on the scriptures there are several reasons why Jesus the son of the living God came to the earth. This is what I call the mission statement of Jesus Christ (John 18:37). You will agree with me that every successful organization, whether a business, family or a group needs a mission statement. Whether it is a formal written statement or simply an informal understanding, a mission statement should clearly define and crystallize the organization's purpose, philosophy and goals. Simply put a mission statement is a business scope clearly showing who you are and what you do. A good mission statement stipulates the following questions: who we are and what we do.

Every person in the organization, from the General Manager or Chief Executive Officer to the cleaner or guard should internalize and understand the statement so that all are working together to accomplish the mission. A mission statement helps keep everyone on course which is important because the organization's product or service or message will grow out its mission statement.

Matthew's gospel records Jesus' well-known Sermon on the Mount in which he states, ***"Do not think that I have come to abolish the Law or the Prophets; I have not come to abolish them but to fulfill them"*** **(Matthew 5:17)**. In this statement Jesus refers to "the Law" and "the Prophets," which is a shorthand way of referring to the Old Testament scriptures. Here we see one of the reasons why Jesus came to the earth: to fulfill the Old Testament.

In other words, Jesus came to fulfill the promises of God that are recorded for us in the Old Testament. And the central promise of the Old Testament is that God would send a descendant of Eve to defeat the devil and reverse the effects of the curse of sin (cf. Genesis 3:15). This descendant would be the Lord's anointed one, the Christ, who would come to save His people from their sin. Jesus came to fulfill this great promise of salvation from God in the Old Testament.

But how will Jesus fulfill this promise? In Mark's gospel, Jesus explains his mission to his disciples right after Peter confesses that Jesus is the Christ (the Messiah). Jesus explains that he "must suffer many things and be rejected by the elders and the chief priests and the scribes and be killed, and after three days rise again" (Mark 8:31). Twice more Jesus tells his disciples that as the Messiah, he has come to be killed and then rise again on the third day (cf. Mark 9:31; 10:33-34).

These are the very events that Christians around the world commemorate and celebrate each year at Easter. But what is the significance of these things? Why did Jesus die on the cross? Jesus' answer is that he *"did not come to be served, but to serve, and to give his life as a ransom for many"*(Mark 10:45). Jesus died on the cross to pay the penalty not for his own sins (for he had none), but to pay the ransom price for the sins of all who believe on him.

One final example of a statement by Jesus about why he came to earth is found in John's gospel: **"For I have come down from heaven not to do my will but to do the will of him who sent me" (John 6:38)**. Jesus came to do the will of his Father in heaven. And what is his Heavenly Father's will? From Isaiah's prophecy concerning the Messiah, we learn that *"it was the Lord's will to crush him and cause him to suffer." Why? Because "the Lord makes his life an offering for sin"* (Isaiah 53:10).

It is the Father's will for Jesus the Messiah to be the substitutionary sacrifice to atone for the sins of his people so that they will be saved from the just wrath of God and raised to eternal life like Jesus was raised. Back in John's gospel Jesus explains it this way: *"And this is the will of him who sent me that I shall lose none of all those he has given me, but raise them up at the last day. For my Father's will is that everyone who looks to the Son and believes in him shall have eternal life, and I will raise them up at the last day"* (John 6:39-40).

The Return of the King and the Kingdom

What is this alternative? It is to return to the original governing concept of God the Creator, which is the kingdom concept. Of course, people who have lived in the context of a democracy or are public all their lives usually find it not only difficult but almost impossible to understand or accept easily this concept of a Kingdom. Compounding the problem is the historical educational process that paints the concept of Kingdoms in a negative light due to experiences with corrupt kings and kingdoms in the past.

As a matter of fact, to many people, in their limited understanding, a Kingdom is simply a dictatorship in the hands of a family. If this is true, then the message of Jesus Christ 2,000 years ago was the promotion and establishment of a dictatorship with Himself as the dictator. He called Himself a "King" and said He came to bring back to earth a "Kingdom." According to this message, which was the only one He preached, the ultimate key to successful human earthly government is the restoration of a King and a Kingdom on earth, one who is righteous, benevolent and a good King. There is only one who can fit that role.

It is the One who created us and designed each one of us with a unique purpose. We must bring back the King. This King cares for His citizens. His rule is a righteous rule. It is this ideal, original kingdom that the heart of all humanity seeks. All of mankind throughout history, and still today, is searching desperately to find that perfect kingdom. Man has tried every imaginable way to create a flawless government. What he has failed to understand is that the original Kingdom, established by the King is what he has been searching for all along.

The Kingdoms of this world must accept the Kingdom of the God and of His Christ. The original and ideal King and Kingdom are superior to all other forms of government. This book will prove that point as we continue our journey to understand this majestic concept. Even within the Church we argue over government, not knowing that there is only one government. We must come to understand the superiority of a kingdom over all other forms of government.

The world needs a benevolent King. We have that King; we just don't recognize Him. I said earlier that one qualification of a legitimate king is ownership of land, which automatically makes him a Lord. God, who has revealed Himself in Jesus Christ, is the ultimate Lord and owner of all things. Who makes God to be King and Lord? Nobody! He is King and Lord by right of creation. Creative rights give Him incontestable ownership rights to earth and the universe. He created all things and that automatically makes Him Lord of all.

We do not give God the earth. He does not need us to make Him King. We can only acknowledge Him as King. His original purpose and plan was to extend His invisible Kingdom of Heaven to earth through His offspring in His image—mankind—and to rule through man as a heavenly agency. In essence, with God's Kingdom on earth, His territory, through all mankind, we would be rulers under the Ruler. Once we are under the rule of this gracious, merciful, benevolent, loving, caring King. He takes personal responsibility for us, not as servants or serfs, but as family and royal children.

This care of the citizens by the king is a concept called "kingdom welfare" describes the king's personal commitment to look after the needs and wants of his citizens within his land. Therefore, the word welfare is a concept that can only be understood fully in the context of a Kingdom. Whenever we submit to a King and his Kingdom, wecome under His welfare. Welfare is not a word that can be used in a democracy. For many, the very word welfare paints negative pictures in their minds, and they believe it to be a societal curse. In the context of a Kingdom, however, welfare is a beautiful word and describes some-thing to be highly desired.

It is a word that is used to express a King's commitment to his citizens. This is why in all kingdoms, the concept of prosperity and national social services is called "commonwealth." Again, this concept can only be understood within the context of a kingdom. In any of the other forms of government, no regime or person has ever been successful in effectively caring for "all" of the citizens. As a matter of fact, even under the best form of human government, democracy, there is the plight of the rich versus the poor, the have's compared to the have not's, the extreme and unequal distribution of wealth, discrimination, racism, divisions, social classifications, and ethnic segregation.

History continually fails to show us a government that manifests the equality, harmony, stability, and community that man has desired and sought after from the day of the fall of Adam. Even our best is defective. No government has been able to take care of its people equally. In a true ideal kingdom, how-ever, all the citizens' welfare is the personal responsibility of the King. This is why the original kingdom concept, as in the Kingdom of God taught by Jesus Christ, is superior to all other governments. Therefore, in a kingdom, the concept of "commonwealth" is also very important, and the word correctly describes the nature of the relationship the king has with his citizens and subjects.

This is the reason why Jesus came to the earth: to save his people from their sins by his life, death and resurrection. His great purpose was to restore sinners back to their God so that they may have eternal life forever with him. And Jesus' great purpose is what gives purpose and meaning to the lives of those who trust in him.

As the Apostle Paul states, ***"And he died for all, that those who live should no longer live for themselves but for him who died for them and was raised again"*** **(2 Corinthians 5:15).**

According to the Gospel of Mathew, when Jesus initiated His public ministry, He made a public statement which He declared for His life: ***"From that time on Jesus began to preach, "Repent, for the kingdom of heaven is near"*** **(Mathew 4:17).**

Jesus came into the world to introduce God's plan for this planet, and the first thing He said was, "Repent!" From this statement Jesus began by telling us that we need to change our minds. That is essentially what the word repent means. Another way of saying this is that we need to change our thinking or our mind – set. ***The Greek word for repent is 'Metanoeo', it means change of mind or purpose.***

So, to repent means to stop, turn around and go in the opposite direction. This is the same when you have taken a wrong direction and turning 180 degree to head in the right direction. This suggests action, but action follows thinking. This means that before we can turn around, we have to decide to turn around why Jesus came to the earth. I want to give you reasons why Jesus was born in Bethlehem 2000 years ago.

Jesus Came to Give His Life as a Ransom for Many

"For even the Son of Man came not to be served but to serve and to give His life a ransom to many". (Mark 10:45).

This passage cuts the heart of why Jesus had to come. He came to give His very life to save ours. He was born into the world so that He could die into the world. Paul has this to say, *"But when the fullness of time had come (that's Christmas) God sent forth His son, born of woman, born under the law, to redeem those who were under the law, so that we might receive adoption as sons" (Gal 4:4-5).*

Jesus redeems us. He pays our debt. But how does Jesus redeem us? He pays with His life. The payment demanded was His sinless life. And that ransom price was impossible for you and me to pay. *The word redeem in the Greek uses the term 'Exagorazo', it means, to buy something out of a market and that item is completely free from the one who sold. That is how free we are after we were redeemed.*

Jesus Came to Call Sinners to Repentance

Jesus answered them, *"It is not the healthy who need a doctor, but the sick. I have not come to call the righteous, but sinners to repentance."*(Luke 5:31-32)

We have hard time thinking about our sin—our disobedience against a blazingly just and holy God—so Jesus uses an image we all understand. He talks about *physical* sickness. Specifically, He compares the sinner to the person who is physical ill and in need of a doctor.

We all know that sickness, like cancer, doesn't just go away if we ignore it. If you have a treatable, yet lethal, form of cancer, and you don't see a doctor for the cure, you will die. The doctor can only save you *if* you go to him. In the same way, we are all sinners in desperate need of salvation, which only comes through repentance and faith in Jesus. Apart from Jesus, we will die in our sins (John 8:24). Only Jesus has the solution—the cure—to our sin problem.

Now that might sound very narrow. And that's because *it is narrow.*

But the truth is *always* narrow. My math students knew this very well. I used to be a full-time high school math and science teacher. If I were to ask my students for the cube root of 27, I would expect a very specific answer. Even though there are an *infinite* number of possible answers, only one is true. The *true* answer is 3. All other numerical answers (e.g. 4, 5, 6, 7) are false.

Jesus is the true solution to our sin problem. In fact, Jesus said, "I am the Way and the Truth and the Life. No one comes to the Father except through me" (John 14:6). Speaking about Jesus, Peter said, "Salvation is found in no one else, for there is no other name under heaven given to mankind by which we must be saved" (Acts 4:12).

Let me anticipate another possible objection. Someone might be thinking, "Well, Tim, maybe I'm like that healthy person who doesn't need a doctor. I'm the righteous person who doesn't need saving." The problem with this belief is that it contradicts both Scripture *and* experience. The Bible says, "For all have sinned and fall short of the glory of God" (Rom. 3:23). How many is *all*? It's all.

But we also know this to be true *apart* from the Bible. We can't even live up to our own standard of morality much less the standard of a perfectly holy God. Remember the ransom has been paid. God has taken the *first step*. Now Jesus is calling sinners to *respond* to that act of grace. Jesus is inviting all people to turn to Him and put their trust in Him.

Jesus Came to Give Eternal Life

For God so loved the world, that he gave his only Son, that whoever believes in Him should not perish but have eternal life."(John 3:16).

Now this is the greatest Christmas gift one can receive—the gift of eternal life. Jesus came to give eternal life *to whoever believes in Jesus*. Eternal life doesn't come *automatically*. You don't get eternal life like you get hair. It only comes once you put your trust in Jesus. You have to *believe in Him*.

It's natural to ask, what happens if I choose *not* to believe in him? Jesus doesn't leave us hanging, He says, ***"Whoever believes in Him is***

not condemned, but whoever does not believe is condemned already, because he has not believed in the name of the only Son of God" (John 3:18).

What does Jesus mean by condemned *already*? The bad news is that we are all sinners and the wages of sin is death. God is an absolutely holy and just Being. He cannot allow sins to go unpunished. In fact, it would be *unjust* for God to allow sinners off scot-free.

There are *two options*: Either you can pay for your sins yourself or you can trust in Jesus' death for the payment of your sins. Reject God's offer of salvation and you will endure eternal punishment. Accept God's offer, and you will have eternal life (Matt. 25:46). It's your choice. But, please know, there is no third option.

So why did Jesus come? Jesus tells us. He came to give His life as a ransom for sinners. He came to call those sinners to repentance. And Jesus came to give eternal life to anyone who would believe in Him. Meditate on these precious theological truths. Allow the purpose of His coming to fill your heart with inexpressible and glorious joy. Joy to the world. The Lord is come.

As we have already seen, repent means "complete change of mind and thinking. The Kingdom of Heaven refers to the sovereign presence and authority of God "invading" and impacting the earthly environment. Jesus challenged His listeners to change from a mind – set that ignored or denied God's Kingdom to one that acknowledged and embraced its arrival.

Jesus's mission was to proclaim the Kingdom of God. He came to restore back the Kingdom that was lost to Satan in the garden of Eden. He came to restore back the lost dominion back to man. He came to restore the lost glory. He came to colonize the earth so that it begins to submit to the Kingdom of God.

From the foregoing, it means that Jesus's assignment was to introduce the Kingdom, He came back to bring to mankind a knowledge of the Kingdom of God, as well as to change our thinking so that we might effectively function in that Kingdom. With a holy passion, Jesus pursued this heavenly assignment. Before He returned to His father, He trained His disciples to continue this mission until its ultimate conclusion.

The wealth in a Kingdom is common. Therefore, in a true ideal Kingdom there isno discrimination or distinction between the rich and the poor, for in such a Kingdom all citizens have equal access to Kingdom wealthand resources provided by the benevolent King. In essence, the King's interest is the welfare of the kingdom and everything in it. If none of the human systems of government are adequate, how then do we adopt God's original Kingdom concept into our world? It begins by understanding the kingdom concept of colonization.

CHAPTER 6

Colonization of the Earth by Our Lord Jesus Christ

When God created the Earth, He shared His governing authority and commissioned mankind to rule and steward what He had made. As His image-bearers, they were to fill the Earth with the kingdom of God, to colonize it with the laws and culture of Heaven. God's plan was for the Earth to be like Heaven.

The Garden of Eden was the first settlement of the colony of Heaven, but the fall changed all that. Through man's sin, his relationship with his kingdom was cut-off and mankind instead began to set up his own rules and way of doing things. The earth-colony was never intended to function without its heavenly governor (the Holy Spirit) giving direction. However, when mankind declared independence, the divine representative from Heaven had to leave. As a result, things went bad.

As highlighted previously, the primary reason for Jesus's coming was to restore the kingdom of God on the Earth. As described in the parable of the evil tenants and the vineyard (Matthew 21:33-44), the King's son and heir was rejected and killed. The kingdom mandate was taken from Israel and given to the Church with a renewed commission to colonize the whole world.

Kingdom colonies were to be established in every nation. Those who became royal citizens of the Kingdom of God (through allegiance to Jesus as their new Lord and King) were legally authorized to teach, with the power of the Governor (the Holy Spirit), the kingdom's laws, customs, language, morals, beliefs, and way of doing things (i.e. the kingdom constitution). This was to impact every place, people, and sphere of society.

However, this is where as the Church we have often missed it historically and even with our practices today! *How* we go about this kingdom expansion (for 'foreign missions' read 'kingdom colonization') is critical. We are NOT to colonize in the way the European nations in the past colonized other countries.

The Church, as the primary agent of God's kingdom, is *not* called to take over a place, people, or area of society and seek to control by force or 'Christian imperialism'. The kingdom of God should never operate from a top-down, control and power basis. Instead, we are to follow the lead of the King Himself and influence through example and service, being 'salt', 'light', and 'yeast'. This is not an easy mandate to fulfill. It will stretch us and challenge our well-established patterns of thought and cultural understanding.

We must remember that God's kingdom can be expressed in many different ways through the diversity of cultures He has made. The kingdom of God transcends all other cultures but doesn't destroy them in the process. We allow God to lead in how our respective cultures can be redeemed to reflect His glory and nature. Instead of making other cultures look like and conform to our ways (ethnocentrism), we impart the blessing of the gospel of the kingdom to them, and allow them to grow into being another unique expression of Christ's kingdom on Earth.

As followers of Jesus we will need to learn the way of the kingdom as modeled by Jesus when He said He only spoke what He heard the Father say, and did only what He saw the Father doing. If we stick to this, we will advance God's kingdom in the way He desires.

How do we pray?

We pray *"Let your kingdom come!"* When Pilate quizzed Jesus about it, Jesus replied: *"My Kingdom is not of this world. If it was, my servants would fight..."* It's an important point. *"We do not wage war as this world does."* And every time you hear of Christians seeking political control or demanding guns to defend their country, you are witnessing a misinterpretation of this verse.

Isaiah offered a wealth of description about the coming Messianic kingdom: *"The government will rest on His shoulders...His ever expanding, peaceful government will never end. He will rule forever with fairness and justice from the throne of His ancestor David. The passionate commitment of the Lord Almighty will guarantee this!"* (9:6-7).

The word "Kingdom" in the original language means "rule" or "reign". God's Kingdom is unique-it is not a human kingdom. Earthly kingdoms rise and fall, but the reign of God will prevail and last forever. God's program involves the rule of righteousness. Jesus told His followers, *"the kingdom of God is within you."* In a spiritual sense, we are living now in the kingdom. Both John the Baptist and Jesus began their ministries announcing that the kingdom of God was "at hand."

It is right here, right now, where Jesus rules.

So why pray that it comes? We are praying that that rule increase and spread, and also, we are anticipating the Wrap-up of History when Jesus returns.

In that sense, as scholars put it: the kingdom is both "already here but not yet fully here."

And we pray in both perspectives. We pray for *"the increase of God's government"* in the present by calling God to bring revival and change the hearts of unbelievers. And this becomes a demand for ethical living on a national, even global scale. How long must we tolerate economic disparity, social injustice and political corruption? Lord, let your kingdom come!

Three words come to mind, as we consider the familiar phrase (though much more could be said). The words are confrontational, prophetic and peaceable.

"*Let your kingdom come!*" is deeply confrontational. We are praying towards a confrontation of two ways of living at odds with each other. We are opposing every worldview that is contrary to God. Prayer is political action and social energy.

David Wells of Gordon-Conwell Seminary calls this kind of prayer a ***"refusal to accept as normal what is pervasively abnormal."*** We see this kind of prayer in what's called the imprecatory psalms, protest songs and prayers that complain about the evil corruption in the world. God welcomes our complaints. Why don't we pray more? We're not angry enough. ***God wants us to process our strong feelings about life through prayer.***

Second, the request is prophetic. That is to say, it considers the world and the time we live in according to the pattern of God's thinking.

History is headed to a climax, a Kingdom-conclusion. How that happens is somewhat debatable (!) but one thing we can know for sure is that God is in control of history. Our task is to wait, watch and to witness. In this sense, our phrase *"Let your kingdom come"* **is much like the final, concluding words of the Bible: *"Come, Lord Jesus"*** (Revelation 22:20).

Third, "Thy kingdom come" is a peaceable prayer. Despite this deep sense of confrontation with a prevailing cultural world view and despite the prophetic insight that God will have his way, the prayer is a prayer for peace. God's Kingdom is a kingdom of peace, for there is no fear or threat in it. Anxiety should be a reminder for us to pray, to *"cast our cares"* on God. When we realize that our sovereign King has things in control, that life has a purpose, that there is a Kingdom apart from our secular culture, we breathe a sigh of relief. Life may seem chaotic, unpredictable, and harsh, but we belong for a Kingdom that will overcome the world.

In Tom Wright's book, *Surprised by Hope: Rethinking Heaven, the Resurrection, and the Mission of the Church,* the resurrection of Jesus is the key starting point of understanding for the prayer of the coming of the Kingdom. The whole book is worth checking out, but here's a clip: "Jesus's resurrection is the beginning of God's new project not to snatch people away from earth to heaven but to colonize earth with the life of heaven. That, after all, is what the Lord's Prayer is about."

Lord, let your Kingdom come! Colonize earth with the life of heaven! I like that! He goes on: "What you do in the present—by painting, preaching, singing, sewing, praying, teaching, building hospitals, digging wells, campaigning for justice, writing poems, caring for the needy, loving your neighbor as yourself—will last into God's future. These activities are not simply ways of making the present life a little less beastly, a little more bearable, until the day when we leave it behind altogether (as the hymn so mistakenly puts it…). They are [just] part of what we may call building for God's Kingdom."Even so, come Lord Jesus.

CHAPTER 7

Introduction of the Royal Governor (The Holy Spirit - Parakletos) to the Earth

We learn from the scriptures that the Spirit of God hovered over the waters that filled the earth. Genesis 1:1-2 (KJV), ***"In the beginning God created the heaven and the earth. And the earth was without form, and void; and darkness was upon the face of the deep. And the Spirit of God moved upon the face of the waters."***

When God began to speak things into existence, it was the Holy Spirit who brought those things to be. The question many often ask is: why should I be filled with the Holy Spirit when I already have a relationship with God? For you to live a genuine Christian life, an authentic life of faith, you need to be filled with the Holy Spirit. Luke 24:49 (KJV), ***"And, behold, I send the promise of my Father upon you: but tarry ye in the city of Jerusalem, until ye be endued with power from on high."***

Jesus commissioned us to be witnesses, and this also calls for us to be filled with the Spirit. You can only be a witness of someone you know, someone you have seen, and those of us in this generation would have been disqualified. But thank God, the Holy Spirit has made it possible for us to be witnesses of Christ, for we know Him after the Spirit.

Notice in the scripture that the first thing mentioned after the reception of power is that we are made witnesses. Acts 1:8 (KJV), ***"But ye shall receive power, after that the Holy Ghost is come upon you: and ye shall be witnesses unto me both in Jerusalem, and in all Judea, and in Samaria, and unto the uttermost part of the earth."*** In legal terms, you can only be witness of something you have seen or heard first-hand with your own ears.

The Holy Spirit is your foremost teacher concerning the things of the kingdom of God. He helps to embed the word of God in our hearts, and helps us to recall the Word we have absorbed in critical moments. John 14:26 (KJV), ***"But the Comforter, which is the Holy Ghost, whom the Father will send in my name, he shall teach you all things, and bring all things to your remembrance, whatsoever I have said unto you."***

The Holy Spirit is described as "another Comforter" (Parakletos in Greek), implying that Jesus was our first comforter. So, what the 12 disciples experienced in Jesus' presence, we can still experience today courtesy of the Holy Spirit.

Holy Spirit is not a name, but an expression of being. He responds to the name of Jesus when you pray. Jesus described the Holy Spirit as "the Spirit of truth". Outside the revelation of the Holy Spirit there is no truth. Desire to be constantly filled with the Holy Spirit. Desire to have a relationship with Him. Desire to fellowship with Him every day. This will help you become fruitful in your walk of faith.

The Holy Spirit is the third Person of the Godhead. He is God. He is not mere feeling or force. In the Bible, He is often referred to as either the Holy Spirit, the Holy Ghost, or simply the Spirit (with capital 'S'). Christian life begins by the Holy Spirit it will also end with the work of the Holy Spirit. In the meantime, the Spirit is working through the believers. Unfortunately, many Christians are yet to learn the truth about the Holy Spirit.

My prayer is that God will use these insights to enlighten you on the purpose and power of the Holy Spirit in your life. And that you will submit to His sanctification work in your life.

The Biblical Truths about the Holy Spirit

The following are just a few of what the Scripture reveals concerning the Holy Spirit:

1. The Holy Spirit is a Divine Person

The Holy Spirit is not mere feeling or force. The Holy Spirit is God. He is expressly declared as a Person in the scriptures. For instance, In the

Gospel of John, Christ refers to Him with possessive pronouns 'He' and 'Him':

John 14:16-17 *"And I will pray the Father, and he shall give you another Comforter, that **he** may abide with you forever; Even the Spirit of truth; whom the world cannot receive, because it seeth him not, neither knoweth him: but ye know him; for he dwelleth with you, and shall be in you."*

John 15:26 *"But when the Comforter is come, whom I will send unto you from the Father, even the Spirit of truth, which proceedeth from the Father, **he** shall testify of me."*

When Christ was giving the outreach instruction at the end of His earthly ministry, He named the Holy Spirit with the Father and the Son:

Matthew 28:19 *Go ye therefore, and teach all nations, baptizing them in the **name of the Father**, and of the **Son**, and of the **Holy Ghost:***

2. He Worked Closely with Christ

The Holy Spirit was the closest companion of Jesus Christ during His earthly life and ministry, from His conception to death and resurrection. The New Testament recognizes the ministry of the Holy Spirit in the life of Christ in the following way:

1. **In Christ's Incarnation – Hebrews 10:5** Wherefore when he cometh into the world, he saith, Sacrifice and offering thou wouldest not, but a body hast thou prepared me
2. **In Christ's Conception – Matthew 1:18** Now the birth of Jesus Christ was on this wise: When as His mother Mary was espoused to Joseph, before they came together, she was found with child of the Holy Ghost.
3. **In Christ's Growth – Luke 2:40 And** the child grew, and waxed strong in spirit, filled with wisdom: and the grace of God was upon him.
4. **In Christ's Baptism – Luke 3:21-22 Now** when all the people were baptized, it came to pass, that Jesus also being baptized, and praying, the heaven was opened, **22** And the Holy Ghost descended in a bodily shape like a dove upon him, and a voice

came from heaven, which said, Thou art my beloved Son; in thee I am well pleased

5. **In Christ's Temptation – Luke 4:14** And Jesus returned in the power of the Spirit into Galilee: and there went out a fame of him through all the region round about.

6. **In Christ's Ministry – Luke 4:18-19 The** Spirit of the Lord *is* upon me, because he hath anointed me to preach the gospel to the poor; he hath sent me to heal the brokenhearted, to preach deliverance to the captives, and recovering of sight to the blind, to set at liberty them that are bruised, **19** To preach the acceptable year of the Lord. See also: **Luke 4:1, 14.**

7. **In Christ's Miracles – Matthew 12:28 But** if I cast out devils by the Spirit of God, then the kingdom of God is come unto you.

8. **In Christ's Sacrifice/Death – Hebrews 9:14 How** much more shall the blood of Christ, who through the eternal Spirit offered himself without spot to God, purge your conscience from dead works to serve the living God?

9. **In Christ's Resurrection – Romans 8:11** But if the Spirit of him that raised up Jesus from the dead dwell in you, he that raised up Christ from the dead shall also quicken your mortal bodies by his Spirit that dwelleth in you.

10. **In Christ Glorification – John 16:14** He shall glorify me: for he shall receive of mine, and shall shew *it* unto you.

Have you ever wondered why God gave us the Holy Spirit when we believed? *If Christ, though He was fully man and fully God during His earthly life and ministry, still depended on the power of the Holy Spirit, how much more do we who are weak in the flesh need the Holy Spirit?* If we recognize our brokenness, and depend on the power of the Holy Spirit, we will experience rapid growth and tremendous fruitfulness in our Christian lives. This is exactly why the Spirit was given to the believer. Ultimately, He will conform us to the image of Christ.

Ephesians 4:12-13 For the perfecting of the saints, for the work of the ministry, for the edifying of the body of Christ: 13 Till we all come in the unity of the faith, and of the knowledge of the Son of God, unto a perfect man, unto the measure of the stature of the fulness of Christ.

3. The Holy Spirit Works through the Word and does not function outside of the Word

John 14:26 But the Comforter, which is the Holy Ghost, whom the Father will send in my name, he shall teach you all things, and bring all things to your remembrance, whatsoever I have said unto you.

The Spirit teaches us all things through the Scriptures, He reveals Christ through the Scriptures inspired by Him. The only way we can glory Christ in our lives is by living according to His will which we cannot learn outside of the Scriptures.

John 14:21, 23 He that hath my commandments, and keepeth them, he it is that loveth me: and he that loveth me shall be loved of my Father, and I will love him, and will manifest myself to him. 23 Jesus answered and said unto him, If a man love me, he will keep my words: and my Father will love him, and we will come unto him, and make our abode with him.

John 15:7 If ye abide in me, and my words abide in you, ye shall ask what ye will, and it shall be done unto you.

1 Peter 1:22 Seeing ye have purified your souls in obeying the truth through the Spirit unto unfeigned love of the brethren, see that ye love one another with a pure heart fervently:

As believers in Christ, the will of God by which we have to live our lives is outlined in the Scriptures which was inspired by the Holy Spirit. According to the Apostle Peter above, we obey the truth only "through the Spirit". It is impossible for you to obey the truth of which you are unaware, and even when you're aware of it, it is still impossible for you to obey it based upon your own strength or discipline.

"For it is God which worketh in you both to will and to do of his good pleasure" (Philippians 2:13). This is the work of the Holy Spirit in the believers' lives.

5. The Spirit Teaches and Speaks to Us through the Word

*John 14:26 But the Comforter, which is the Holy Ghost, whom the Father will send in my name, **he shall teach you all things**, and **bring all things to your remembrance, whatsoever I have said unto you**.*

1 John 2:24, 27 Let that therefore abide in you, which ye have heard from the beginning. If that which ye have heard from the beginning shall remain in you, ye also shall continue in the Son, and in the Father. 27 But the anointing which ye have received of him abideth in you, and ye need not that any man teach you: but as the same anointing teacheth you of all things, and is truth, and is no lie, and even as it hath taught you, ye shall abide in him.

2 Timothy 3:15 And that from a child thou hast known the holy scriptures, which are able to make thee wise unto salvation through faith which is in Christ Jesus.

6. You Cannot Be Filled by the Spirit If you are Devoid of the Word

If the Holy Spirit works through the Scriptures and you cannot obey the truth that you have not learned, then the Holy Spirit will not work in you if you're not conversant with the Word. This makes sense since yielding requires that you know the commandments to which you are to yield, and it gives way to the move and filling of the Spirit. This does not mean that a believer who is devoid of the Scriptures does not have indwelling Spirit, it just means that the Spirit is yet to be in control of his or her life. To be filled with the Spirit is to be full of the truth of Christ which will in turn produces the desire to live for Him. This point is the reason for Colossians 3:16-17:

Colossians 3:16-17 Let the word of Christ dwell in you richly in all wisdom; teaching and admonishing one another in psalms and hymns and spiritual songs, singing with grace in your hearts to the Lord. 17 And whatsoever ye do in word or deed, do all in the name of the Lord Jesus, giving thanks to God and the Father by him.

7. The Holy Spirit Functions in Salvation

John MacArthur writes in *Strange Fire,* "The genuine purpose and power of His [The Holy Spirit] ministry: freeing sinners from death, giving them everlasting life, regenerating their hearts, transforming their nature, empowering them for spiritual victory, confirming their place in the family of God, interceding for them according to the will of God, sealing them securely for their eternal glory, and promising to raise them to immortality in the future."

According to **Ephesians 1:13**, no one can be saved without first hearing and believing the Word of truth. This is the same truth which is revealed by the Holy Spirit. He inspired the Word of truth:

2 Peter 1:19-21 We have also a more sure word of prophecy; whereunto ye do well that ye take heed, as unto a light that shineth in a dark place, until the day dawn, and the day star arise in your hearts: 20 Knowing this first, that no prophecy of the scripture is of any private interpretation. 21 For the prophecy came not in old time by the will of man: but holy men of God spake as they were moved by the Holy Ghost.

Hebrews 4:12 For the word of God is quick, and powerful, and sharper than any two-edged sword, piercing even to the dividing asunder of soul and spirit, and of the joints and marrow, and is a discerner of the thoughts and intents of the heart.

Also, the Bible says concerning the Holy Spirit that He is the One who helps the sinner to obey the truth:

1 Peter 1:22 Seeing ye have purified your souls in obeying the truth through the Spirit unto unfeigned love of the brethren, see that ye love one another with a pure heart fervently.

He is also the One who illuminates the truth of the scripture in the heart of the believers.

8. The Spirit proceeds in convicting the sinners in three areas as outlined by Christ in **John 16:7-11**

Nevertheless, I tell you the truth; It is expedient for you that I go away: for if I go not away, the Comforter will not come unto you; but if I depart, I will send him unto you. 8 And when he is come, he will **reprove the world of sin, and of righteousness, and of judgment:** *9 Of sin, because they believe not on me; 10 Of righteousness, because I go to my Father, and ye see me no more; 11 Of judgment, because the prince of this world is judged.*

1. **He reproves the world of sin**, revealing their sinfulness and the wages of sin – **John 8:24** I said therefore unto you, that ye shall die in your sins: for if ye believe not that I am *he*, ye shall die in your sins.

2. **He reproves the world of righteousness**, enlightening them to their need for God's righteousness – **Romans 3:10** As it is written, there is none righteous, no, not one:

3. **He reproves the world of judgment**, warning them of the consequences of rejecting the gospel – **2 Corinthians 4:4** In whom the god of this world hath blinded the minds of them which believe not, lest the light of the glorious gospel of Christ, who is the image of God, should shine unto them.

After heartily receiving the truth of the gospel, the Holy Spirit regenerates the sinful heart, converting them from being dead in sin to being alive in Christ:

Ephesians 2:4-6 But God, who is rich in mercy, for his great love wherewith he loved us, 5 Even when we were dead in sins, hath quickened us together with Christ, (by grace ye are saved;) 6 And hath raised us up together, and made us sit together in heavenly places in Christ Jesus

Titus 3:4-7 But after that the kindness and love of God our Saviour toward man appeared, 5 Not by works of righteousness which we have done, but according to his mercy he saved us, by the washing of regeneration, and renewing of the Holy Ghost; 6 Which he shed on us abundantly through Jesus Christ our Saviour; 7 That being justified by his grace, we should be made heirs according to the hope of eternal life.

2 Corinthians 5:17 Therefore if any man be in Christ, he is a new creature: old things are passed away; behold, all things are become new.

The principal purpose of the Holy Spirit is to point the world to Christ **(John 14:26,16:14; 1 John 4:2-3)** and in turn conform them to the image of Christ.

9. **The Holy Spirit is Building the Church**

The Holy Spirit forms and is still building up the believers today. The Spirit regenerates and baptizes all believers into one Body according to *1 Corinthians 12:12-13, For as the body is one, and hath many members, and all the members of that one body, being many, are one body: so also, is Christ. 13 For by one Spirit are we all baptized into one body, whether we be Jews or Gentiles, whether we be bond or free; and have been all made to drink into one Spirit.*

10. **The Holy Spirit also imparts gifts for service to every member of that Body of Christ.**

1 Corinthians 12:7-11 But the manifestation of the Spirit is given to every man to profit withal. 8 For to one is given by the Spirit the word of wisdom; to another the word of knowledge by the same Spirit; 9 To another faith by the same Spirit; to another the gifts of healing by the same Spirit; 10 To another the working of miracles; to another prophecy; to another discerning of spirits; to another divers kinds of tongues; to another the interpretation of tongues: 11 But all these worketh that one and the selfsame Spirit, dividing to every man severally as he will.

1. **The Spirit empowers the believers to serve:**

Acts 1:8 But ye shall receive power, after that the Holy Ghost is come upon you: and ye shall be witnesses unto me both in Jerusalem, and in all Judaea, and in Samaria, and unto the uttermost part of the earth.

2. **The Spirit also provides guidance in Christian service**

Acts 16:6 Now when they had gone throughout Phrygia and the region of Galatia, and were forbidden of the Holy Ghost to preach the word in Asia.

3. **The Holy Spirit gathersbelievers and make them the temple of God.**

1 Corinthians 3:16-17 Know ye not that ye are the temple of God, and that the Spirit of God dwelleth in you? 17 If any man defile the temple of God, him shall God destroy; for the temple of God is holy, which temple ye are."
This should not be confused with the temple of God in individual believer as in
2 Corinthians 6:16 And what agreement hath the temple of God with idols? for ye are the temple of the living God; as God hath said, I will dwell in them, and walk in them; and I will be their God, and they shall be my people.

4.   The Holy Spirit is the Sealer of the Believers

Ephesians 1:13-14 In whom ye also trusted, after that ye heard the word of truth, the gospel of your salvation: in whom also after that ye believed, ye were sealed with that holy Spirit of promise, 14 Which is the earnest of our inheritance until the redemption of the purchased possession, unto the praise of his glory.

Believers are guaranteed eternal security. We can never lose our salvation. The Bible says that those whom God predestinated, called, and justified, He also glorified. This is a done deal. Christ confirms this Himself:

John 10:27-30 My sheep hear my voice, and I know them, and they follow me: 28 And I give unto them eternal life; and they shall never perish, neither shall any man pluck them out of my hand. 29 My Father, which gave them me, is greater than all; and no man is able to pluck them out of my Father's hand. 30 I and my Father are one.

Romans 8:35-39 Who shall separate us from the love of Christ? shall tribulation, or distress, or persecution, or famine, or nakedness, or peril, or sword? 36 As it is written, For thy sake we are killed all the day long; we are accounted as sheep for the slaughter. 37 Nay, in all these things we are more than conquerors through him that loved us. 38 For I am persuaded, that neither death, nor life, nor angels, nor principalities, nor powers, nor things present, nor things to come, 39 Nor height, nor depth, nor any other creature, shall be able to separate us from the love of God, which is in Christ Jesus our Lord.

The reality of this is brought to light by the Scripture. The presence of the Holy Spirit in us is proof that we belong to God (**1 John 4:4**), that we are secured by God (**Romans 8:9-11; 2 Corinthians 5:5**), and that God will still return to take us home (**John 14:3**). The Spirit is named the earnest [down payment] of our inheritance (**Ephesians 1:13-14; 2 Corinthians 1:20-22**), and we are sealed by Him until our glorification, "the redemption of the purchased possession".

Part III

THE KINGDOM KEYS FOR SUCCESS

CHAPTER 8

The Concept of Keys

One day Jesus said, "My Father has given you the knowledge of the secrets of the Kingdom. I will teach you how to use the keys." Jesus left no doubt that the Kingdom was supposed to work for His ecclesia just as it worked for Him, for on the night before His death He told them: I tell you the truth, anyone who has faith in Me will do what I have been doing. He will do even greater things than these, because I am going to the Father. And I will do whatever you ask in my name, so that the Son may bring glory to the Father. You may ask Me for anything in my name, and I will do it (John 14:12-14). Jesus' ecclesia (which includes us as the Body of Christ – the Corpus Christi) was going to do the same things He was doing—and more—because the Holy Spirit who would come after He was gone would teach them the keys of the Kingdom and how to use them. One significant key is embedded in this passage: the key to opening the "warehouse" of Heaven. The key that opens that lock is prayer—asking in Jesus' name—and whatever and any thing we ask will be done.

That is a wide-open promise, but it is not a way to gratify our own selfish wants and desires. We must use the right key. We must ask in Jesus' name—according to His will and in line with His purpose. That is what will open Heaven's flood-gates. The twelve disciples of Jesus had already seen this key activated in unforgettable fashion the day Jesus fed five thousand people with fives loaves of bread and two fish. The crowd had been with Jesus all day listening to His teaching. Now it was late in the day, and they were hungry.

Jesus' disciples suggested He send them away into the villages to get food, but Jesus has another idea. He was preparing to teach them how to use a key: Jesus replied, "They do not need to go away. You give them something to eat." "We have here only five loaves of bread and two fish," they answered. "Bring them here to Me," He said. And He directed the people to sit down on the grass. Taking the five loaves and the two fish and looking up to heaven, He gave thanks and broke the loaves.

Then He gave them to the disciples, and the disciples gave them to the people. They all ate and were satisfied, and the disciples picked up twelve baskets of broken pieces that were left over. The number of those who ate was about five thousand men, besides women and children (Matthew14:16-21 emphasis added).

Jesus used this situation to test His disciples to see if they picked up on the secrets. He said, "You feed them." That was the test. They should have asked, "Which key do we use?" Instead, they said, "All we have is...." They were limited by what they could see. But in the kingdom of God, we walk not by sight but by faith. The lesson Jesus wanted them (and us) to learn is that when you know the Keys to the kingdom secrets, you will never again say, "All I have is...."Look at the progression: Jesus looked up toward heaven and gave thanks.

He put in the key of prayer and unlocked the ware-house. Then He broke the bread, gave it to His disciples, and they distributed it among the people. It should work for us the same way. Through prayer in Jesus' name (the key), we unlock Heaven's ware-house. The King Himself draws forth from its abundance and gives it to us, and we then give it to others. But we have to know the key that opens the warehouse. That knowledge is Christ's promise to us: "The knowledge of the secrets of the kingdom of God has been given to you."

Principles of Keys

Knowledge leads to understanding. Once we know the principles behind keys, we can understand how they work in the Kingdom. There are several principles that define the properties of keys.

1.   Keys represent authority

If you possess a key to a place, it means you have access to that place. Suppose your boss entrusts you with a key to the store or the office. By doing so, he shows not only that he trusts you but also that he has delegated a certain amount of authority to you. The key to your house means you have authority there. The key to your car gives you authority to drive whenever you want to. Christ says, "I am giving you the keys of the Kingdom of Heaven. I am giving you authority in heaven, the same authority I have." What an awesome gift! Few of us have done more than just scratch the surface in learning what this means.

2.   Keys represent access.

A key gives you instant access to everything that key opens. The secret is in knowing what the key opens. The keys of the Kingdom of God give us immediate access to all the resources of heaven. But we have to know how to use them. So often we limit ourselves by trusting or believing only in what we can see with our eyes or reason out with our minds. A Kingdom mind-set completely changes our perspective. When a pagan king sent his army to capture the Hebrew Prophet Elisha, the prophet's servant was terrified one morning to find the army surrounding the city."Oh, my lord, what shall we do?" the servant asked."Don't be afraid," the prophet answered. "Those who are with us are more than those who are against us." And Elisha prayed, "O Lord, open his eyes so he may see."

Then the Lord opened the servant's eyes, and he looked and saw the hills full of horses and chariots of fire all around Elisha. As the enemy came down toward him, Elisha prayed to the Lord, "Strike these people with blindness." So, he struck them with blindness, as Elisha had asked (2 Kings 6:15b-18). Elisha's servant was frightened by what he saw around him, but he didn't have a key. Elisha had a key, unlocked heaven, and brought down an angelic host to protect them. The prophet tapped into a principle that took him to a system that made that pagan army look like toy soldiers by comparison. When you have the keys of the Kingdom, you have no lack and no crisis because the King is greater than them all. Jesus said He would teach us to walk in that kind of authority, access, and confidence.

3.   Keys represent ownership

Possession of a key gives you de facto ownership of whatever that key opens. Therefore, when you possess the keys of the Kingdom of heaven, you have ownership of heaven on earth. Jesus said, "Whatever you bind on earth will be bound in heaven, and whatever you loose on earth will be loosed in heaven." In other words, you own on earth whatever is going on in Heaven. This means that you should never judge how your life is going simply by your circumstances. Suppose you get laid off from your job.

It would be easy to get scared and stressed out because you have a family and bills to pay and no money. That's your circumstances. As a Kingdom citizen with the keys of the kingdom, however, you have ownership of heaven on earth. You can be confident and even rejoice in the prospect of a bright future because you have a source of supply and provision that those outside the Kingdom cannot even conceive. So, go have a prosperity party! The King is preparing to bless and prosper you from a completely unexpected direction. When you "co-own" the sources of the King, you are never destitute.

4. Keys represent control

If you possess the key to something, you control it. You control when it opens, when it closes, and who gets access to it. A key helps you control time. In other words, you decide whether to open it up at 8:00 or 10:00 or 6:00 or whenever. This gives you control when something comes. If you need something now, you operate a key. One day the Hebrew prophet Elijah met a poor widow gathering sticks at the town gate. This was during a severe drought. He asked her for a drink of water and a piece of bread. "As surely as the Lord your God lives," she replied, "I don' thave any bread— only a handful of flour in a jar and a little oil in a jug. I am gathering a few sticks to take home and make a meal for myself and my son, that we may eat it—and die." Elijah said to her, "Don't be afraid.

Go home and first make a small cake of bread for me from what you have and bring it to me, and then make something for yourself and your son. For this is what the Lord, the God of Israel says: 'The jar of flour will not be used up and the jug of oil will not run dry until the day the Lord gives rain on the land.'" She went away and did as Elijah had told her. So, there was food every day for Elijah and for the woman and her family. For the jar of flour was not used up and the jug of oil didnot run dry, in keeping with the word of the Lord spoken by Elijah (1 Kings 17:12-16).

The truth of the widow's circumstances was that she and her son were about to starve. Elijah approaches and makes a bold request that even sounds selfish: "I know you don't have much, but feed me first and then yourself and your son. Trust in the Lord; He will take care of you." This was not selfishness. Elijah was offering the woman a key. Once she took it, she had control. By faith and obedience, she unlocked heaven's ladder and brought down for herself and her family supernatural provision that sustained them until the drought ended.

Her entire life and mind-set shifted from the circumstances of want and privation to a Kingdom perspective of unlimited abundance.

5. Keys represent power

Whoever gives you keys gives you power at the same time. This is similar to control. You have control—power—over whatever you possess the Keys for. If you know how to use the keys, whatever they unlock is at your disposal. The Keys to your house give you the power to come and go and to allow or disallow others to enter. When Jesus gave us the keys to the kingdom, He gave us power in Heaven. Whatever we bind one art that affects Heaven; whatever we loose on earth affects Heaven; whatever we close on earth, Heaven closes.

Do we really have that much power as kingdom citizens? Yes the King does not want us to live as victims of the earth's system, so He has given us the ability to tap into a realm that is invisible but absolutely real and can literally affect the physical earth. This is why Christ was able to live an abundant life in times of crisis. He had power from Heaven. And He has given that power to us.

7. Keys represent freedom

When you have keys, you are free to go in and out. You are free to lock and un lock, to open and close. The keys of the kingdom give us freedom from fear and all the other limiting emotions of an earthly system. I used to wonder why Jesus was so carefree, so calm, and so in control no matter what was happening around Him. It was because He had the Key of freedom. One day Jesus was asleep in the back of a boat while His cabinet (some of whom were fishermen) sailed it across the Sea of Galilee. As happens frequently on that body of water, a severe storm blew up suddenly.

The storm was so fierce that even the experienced sailors aboard feared that the boat was going to sink. How could Jesus sleep through such a crisis? Their lives were in danger, and He was snoozing in the stern! The disciples went and woke Him, saying, "Lord, save us! We are going to drown!" He replied, "You of little faith, why are you so afraid?" Then He got up and rebuked the wind sand the waves, and it was completely calm. The men were amazed and asked, "What kind of man is this? Even the winds and the waves obey Him!" (Matthew 8:25-27).Jesus said, "You of little faith, why are you so afraid?"

In essence He was saying, "What's the matter? Where are your keys?" Then He took out a key, locked up the storm, and it stopped. In amazement, the disciples asked, "What kind of man is this?" Just a man with Keys. The keys of the Kingdom are the keys to ultimate truth, the knowledge of which brings true liberty. Jesus said: If you hold to my teaching, you are really My disciples.

Then you will know the truth, and the truth will set you free (John 8:31b-32).By "teaching," Jesus is not referring so much to Scripture verses as much as the principles, laws, and precepts contained in those verses. Freedom comes in knowing the truth. Truth alone is not what sets you free. What sets you free is the truth you know. The keys of the Kingdom can bring you into the knowledge of the truth.

Characteristics of Keys

1. Keys are laws

They are fixed, reliable standards thatnever change. When used correctly, they always work.

2. Keys are principles

When Jesus spoke of "the keys of the kingdom," He wasn't talking about literal physical keys toopen physical locks. The keys of the kingdom are principles, systems that operate under fixed laws. When Hegives us the keys, He gives us the principles by which the kingdom of God operates. We gain access to the systems that make the kingdom of God work. And oncewe learn the laws, the system, and the principles, all ofheaven will be available to us.

3.   Keys are systems

Every government runs on systems: the social system, the economic system, the political system, the educational system, the telecommunications system, etc. Knowledge of the systems and how they work is a Key to power and influence. Control the systems and you control the government. Disrupt the systems and you disrupt the government. Destroy the systems and you destroy the nation. That is how powerful systems are.

Even more, that is how powerful knowledge can be. The systems of the kingdom of God are beyond the reach of those outside the kingdom and are in no danger of being disrupted or destroyed. Kingdom citizens, on the other hand, have access to those systems and can bring the influence of kingdom systems to bear in earthly situations. That is why kingdom citizens can rest confident in victory and success no matter what circumstances may suggest. So, the most important thing any of us could do is to make sure that we are citizens of the kingdom of God.

4.   Keys activate function

A car operates on gasoline. The "Key" of gasoline activates the function of the car. Without gasoline, the car will not run no matter how many other keys you have. Likewise, a radio with no receiver cannot fulfill its function of converting radio waves into audible sound waves for you to hear. The "Key" of a receiver is missing, and without it, the radio is only an empty, silent box. The box may be pretty, the glass clean and shiny, but it cannot fulfill its purpose because the key to activate its function is not there. Tome, religion is like that attractive radio or that stylish but gas-less car that does not work. Like them, religion may look beautiful and impressive on the outside withal its regalia and traditions, but it has no keys and therefore lacks the ability and the power to activate kingdom function.

The keys of the kingdom activate Heaven so that we can fully enjoy our rights and privileges as kingdom citizens. This is far more sure and secure than depending on the systems of the world for our enjoyment. On this point, kingdom ambassador Paul counsels: Command those who are rich in this present world not to be arrogant nor to put their hope in wealth, which is so uncertain, but to put their hope in God, who richly provides us with everything for our enjoyment(1 Timothy 6:17).The keys of the kingdom allow us to enjoy all the rich and good things of God without measure.

5. Keys initiate action

Just as the key to a car initiates action by starting the engine, the keys of the Kingdom, when we know how to use them, initiate action in Heaven.

6. Keys are the principles by which the Kingdom of God operates

Not only are keys principles, but specifically, keys to the operation of the kingdom. They give us access to the blueprints, the schematic, and the flowcharts so that we can understand and appropriate the inner workings of the kingdom of God.

7. Keys cannot be substituted by feelings, emotions, wishful thinking, or manipulation

If you are locked out of your house without a key, no amount of begging or pleading or wishing will make that door open. If your car is out of gas, you can sit behind the wheel and dream and will all you want for it to move, but it will stay right where it is. Religion is built on feelings, emotions, wishful thinking, and manipulation. It is different with the kingdom. The Kingdom of God operates on keys. You can wish and feel and beg and plead all you want, but without the right Keys, you will still be locked out of all the things God promised you because feelings do not open doors. Keys do.

In the world's system, you get ahead by killing, robbing, hurting, manipulating, climbing up on people, and using people, stealing, gambling— any way you can. But in the kingdom of God, everything is reversed. To get ahead, you must do the opposite of what you do in the world. Instead of getting, you give; instead of hoarding, you release; instead of grabbing, you give up; instead of hating, you love; instead of every-man-for-himself, you show first regard to others. Yes, this is counterintuitive, but that is the way God's Kingdom works.

CHAPTER 9

Understanding the Place of Success

Let me start by saying success is the function of a dream. Just as life, success does not come by chance. Remember that man is composed of body, soul and spirit. The soul is your mind. There is something you visualize in your mind and keep wanting to achieve irrespective of challenges. That is what I call your dream. If you do not have a dream, then you cannot achieve anything in life. Success can be predictable. So too failure can be predictable.

Many scholars say that success is about crafting goals and making plans to achieve them. This means that success is not about comparing you with what others have done but comparing with your own achievements. Achieving your dream (what you were born to do) and be on top performance in life is based on obedience to principles.

The Principles of Success

The principle of prayer and fasting

Prayer and fasting are the mightiest tools God gave to man. To pray is to commune with God. You need prayer to be successful. Remember that the ONE who is for you is more than the ones against you. Go into your closet, pray believing that you have received.

Acts 13:2, 3

2 *"As they ministered to the Lord, and they fasted, the Holy Ghost said, "Separate me Barnabas and Saul for the work whereunto I have called them"* (Acts 13:2). 3 "And when they had fasted and prayed and laid their hands on them they sent them away."

The above scripture shows the power and the importance of prayer and fasting. At the Church at Antioch, after certain prophets and teachers; such as Barnabas and Simeon that was called Niger, Lucius of Cyrene and Manaen, which had been brought up with Herod the Tetrarch and Saul the Holy Spirit instructed them to separate Barnabas and Saul for the work God had called them.

Understand the Kingdom Laws

Every kingdom has its own laws and the word of a king in a kingdom becomes law. Let us look at what God the King of Kings, Lord of Lords is saying to Joshua.

"This book of the law shall not depart out of thy mouth; but thou shalt meditate therein day and night, that thou mayest observe to do according to all that is written therein: for then thou shalt make thy way prosperous and then thou shalt have good success". **(Joshua 1:8)**

It is said that those that run with principles emerge high flyers in life.

"And it shall come to pass, if thou shalt hearken diligently unto the voice of the LORD thy God, to observe and to do all his commandments which I command thee this day, that the LORD thy God will set thee on high above all nations of the earth"(Deuteronomy 28:1).

Based on the above scripture it means that you do not have to go around experimenting things; just learn to exercise the principles that surround success in your domain. If you know someone who knows the way you need to rise up and begin to follow him or her. Some of these people can become your mentors in life.

The principle of passion

Many people do not have passion. Passion is an inner urge that does not care what the external senses detect. It is that energy created by a purpose and meaning for life. It is a commitment that is beyond contention. Nothing can stop you from achieving the thing you visualize.

When you figure out something you can genuinely die for, then you have passion; then you have started living. If what you are doing is something you can stop doing and still be happy, then you have not figured out your purpose and passion.

Dr Myles Munroe says "What we need are not jobs; we need assignments in life". Figure out your purpose and passion! What is that thing you are not satisfied because you are not doing yet? What is that thing you really want to do genuinely? That is your passion; go for it and remember that all things are possible for they that believe. If the opinions of the crowd still matter to you then you do not know your passion. If you die without having done this thing then you won't have done something for humanity.

Building Successful Relationships

If you observe in the scriptures Aaron followed Moses, Elisha followed Elijah, Paul followed Gamaliel, Timothy, Titus and Philemon followed Paul, Peter, James and John followed Jesus. No one does it alone in life. This is what I call the power of connection.

Ecclesiastes 4:9,10

9 "Two are better than one; because they have a good reward for their labour" 10 "For if they fall, the one will lift up his fellow: but woe to him that is alone when he falleth; for he hath not another to help him up."

It is possible to get some results without relating but you get better results when you find a good relationship. Someone said "You are going to be the same person you are today in five years except for the books you read and the people you walk with." So, no relationship leaves you neutral. You are either made or marred by the relationship you find yourself

"He that walketh with the wise men shall be wise but a companion of fools shall be destroyed" **(Proverbs 13:20)**

Abraham's vision was delayed because of the presence of Lot and Terah. Until Terah died and Lot was separated from him, Abraham did not enjoy speed in the pursuit of his vision. Everyone has the responsibility to decide who to walk with since friendship is by choice, not by force. This is a call to look around you and study those who have succeeded in life and those who think they have failed. You will notice that there is something successful people share in common and likewise those who think they have already failed.

Genesis 12:4 says, *"And Lot went with him...."* and somewhere on the way they went into conflicts. Look at Gen 13:14-15. Your destiny is inched in building successful relationships. Psalm 1:1 says, **"Blessed is the man that walketh not in the counsel of the ungodly nor standeth in the way of sinners nor sitteth in the seat of scornful."** A man who keeps good company will never run dry and will never wither.

The principle of purpose

Purpose is a clear guiding vision for your life. If you do not know your purpose, anything is right for you. How misleading! Without a vision, you do not have any self-imposed standards (self-discipline) for your life. Purpose is the original intent of your creation. Notice that you have a unique thumb print. Even identical twins are not identical. Everybody is unique by their creation. *If you are so unique in your creation, it is because there is something only you can do.* The thing God created you to do is purpose.

When you figure it out, that is vision. Joseph understood his purpose and saw the vision of his life very clearly. That is why he was rejected, and that might happen to you too. Notwithstanding, do not yield to the pressure. Believe in what you imagine yourself becoming; it is real! To stand out and keep to your vision generally defiles people's expectations of you. Those who think they know you so very well will try telling you that that is something no one has ever done, so you cannot. Do not yield to that. There is something you were created to do in life; figure it out.

The principle of planning

In planning we talk about 6 Ps: Prior, Proper, Planning Prevents, Poor Performance. It goes without saying that if you fail to plan, you plan to fail. If you do not have a plan, you will fail. Plan your work, work your plan. Without a plan you function with the wind; left and right, up and down doing anything and everything. The heart of man makes its plan and God directs it. Plan your day, plan your week, and establish a plan for each month. Take care of the seconds and the minutes and hours will take care of themselves.

The principle of persistence

Persistence is the consistent insistence that you have what you are after. To be persistent is to refuse to stop no matter the challenges. For how long have you been after your dream? It is not because it failed the last time that it will fail this time. Just keep on keeping on until the day breaks and the shadows flee away. Winners never quit, and quitters never win. Do not give up, never give up!

CHAPTER 10

Discovering the God's Purpose for Your Life

In this chapter let me start by saying Dr. Myles Munroe a renowned minister of the gospel who went to be with the Lord in 2014 taught on this subject of discovering God's purpose for our lives very well. Dr. Myles Munroe said the richest place in the world is not the South Africa's gold mine, it is not the Nigeria Oil wells, it is not the United States of America's silver mine but rather it is the CEMETERY. The cemetery contains millions of ideas, visions and dreams that were not fulfilled. It contains books that were not written, songs that were not sung, cars that were not manufactured, buildings and towers that were not built. The greatest tragedy in life is not death, the greatest tragedy in life is a life without a purpose. A dead man is no long accountable to why he is breathing but you who are living must give account. God's greatest desire is for you to discover your purpose for life.

Proverbs 19:21 **"Many are the plans in the man's heart but it is the Lord's purpose/counsel that will stand".**

To God, this verse means 3 things;

1. Purpose is more important than plans
2. Purpose is more powerful than plans
3. Purpose precedes plans.

God says your plans for life, your ideas, your dreams, desired career, your business, what you want to study in college should come after discovering His purpose for your life. God is therefore only concerned with your purpose and not your plans.

What is purpose? Purpose is:

1. The original intent for a thing.
2. The reason why a thing was made.
3. The cause for creation.

Purpose is the reason why a thing exists, it is the desired result for a thing, it is the source of destiny. The intent of God is the will of God. God is pleased when you discover your purpose for life and get busy doing it. God is only committed to His purpose and not your plans. Whatever God calls for, He provides for. Whatever you were born to do, is already paid for. Wealth will surely come your way when you pursue the project of God for your life hence your money should be used to finance God's project in your life. Until you find why God made you, you will never have meaning in life.

PURPOSE IS YOUR LIFE. Ephesians 1:3

"The Father has already blessed us with all spiritual blessings in the Heavenly places."

The only issue here is that it is trapped in the unseen realm. Whatsoever you need to succeed has already been made available. Our spiritual blessings in the Heavenly places will only come when it sees the reason why it exists; It exists because God chose you!

Purpose Attracts Provision!!!

When you look into what you are born to do, God releases the required resources you need to do it. If you discover the assignment of why God chose you, then everything you need will surely find you. Your provision comes when you discover your assignment. What you are born to do will attract what has been hiding from you. Your purpose is the key to the wealth of your country. Your past, present does not depict your figure. You do not need to leave your country to find God's will for your life nor to finance it. There is a reason why He has placed you in that Nation. You do not need to leave home to change the world, when you find your purpose, the World will come to you.

How do you attract what's trapped in the unseen realm?

You have got to obey God. You have got to understand that the work God has given to you is a baby (Pregnancy) and you are a virgin because you have never done it before. You therefore need His leading and guidance. You have to involve the Spirit of God (Holy Spirit), God will never give you an assignment that does not involve Him.

For if you can succeed in what you are doing without God, then it is not a godly thing. You need to be around people who will make your baby leap (Mary and Elizabeth). Do not keep company with barren people who are trying to talk you out of your dream. "Show me your friends and I will tell you your future" Choose people who will help you get to where God wants you to be. Keep company with people with vision, people who are also carrying a dream. Make a choice to be purpose-driven today.

The Principles of Purpose

Many ministry commentators such as Dr. Myles Munroe say that principles are like light houses. They are laws that cannot be broken. We can only break ourselves against them. Just as Law or Principle of Universal Gravitation both governs and exhibits the attraction between the earth and the moon, so the principles of purpose both rule and make known the function of purpose.

Here are few principles of purpose that have been tested by different men of God. The first principle of purpose is that God is a God of purpose. It goes without saying that every creator or manufacturer begins with purpose. He first establishes his intent before beginning the process of production. God is therefore the source of purpose. Nature is filled with evidence that He determines the purpose for a thing before He creates it. This means that God did not make anything for the fun of it. Yes, he never created something just to see if He could make it. The truth is that before creative act ever takes place, God has in His mind the why and the how of what He decides to make. He does everything with and for a purpose.

The second principle is that everything in life has a purpose. If God is a God of purpose and He created everything, then everything in life has a purpose. This amazes everyone. I would like to point out that the rat, the lice, the mosquitoes, the birds, the ants and even the snakes we fear were made by God to fulfill a specific purpose. Just because we do not understand a creature's purpose does not mean that it is purposeless. Our reactions of fear do not negate their reasons for existence, because everything serves a purpose. ***In essence, ignorance of purpose does not cancel purpose.***

The third principle is that, not every person is known. Our world is plagued by the desire to have more and more. Many people argue that having something is not really the important thing. Knowing the reason for what you have is much more important. You can agree with me that there are times, however, when the why is not known. This does not mean that the thing, event or person does not have a purpose; its purpose just is not known.

The fourth principle is that whenever purpose is not known, abuse is inevitable. Abuse occurs whenever we do not use something according to its creator's intentions. In other words, if you do not know the purpose for something you cannot do anything other than abuse it. This means that no matter how good your intentions may be, they are cancelled by your ignorance. The word abuse can be defined as "abnormal use." In other words, if you do not know the proper use for something, you will use it in disorderly manner. Unknown purpose also leads to misuse, which is a stronger form of abuse. To misuse something means that you miss the intended use.

The fifth principle of purpose is that the purpose is only found in the mind of a creator. A created thing cannot know what the mind of the creator is when he planned and built it. The same principle is true for any product. If you want to know the purpose of a product, you must ask the manufacturer or his authorized representative. The product itself cannot tell you. That is why most manufacturers put a label somewhere on their products or they give you similar information in a manual.

Purpose and Vision

Dr. Myles Munroe in his book: In pursuit of purpose points out that purpose gives precision to life. This means that life with purpose is precise and directed. So is a true saying that life without purpose is depressing. Purpose provides vision.

"*Where there is no vision, the people perish....*" (Proverbs 29:18).

This is true because purpose provides a reason for existence. It encourages maximized performance toward an intended result. To say in another way, purpose is destination thus the end toward which something exists and predestination thus going back to start after seeing the outcome. When you know the desired end before you begin the journey, you are much more likely to stick with your task and stay on the prescribed path. This means that vision is the direct result of purpose, providing the impetus to act on the direction set by purpose. Vision sets goals, which motivate a plan of action.

The primary value of purpose is the translation of vision derived from purpose into a plan of action. This occurs through the setting of specific goals. The presence of goals allows for both the development of a plan and the effective use of energy as all efforts are put into fulfillment of the purpose. Purpose protects you from being busy but not effective. Goals are steps toward a desired end. They create priorities, determine decisions, dictate companions and predict choices. Together they form preferred flight plan to the desired destination.

The Benefits of Purpose

There are five benefits of purpose. So is a true saying that without purpose, life is subjective. ***First, purpose gives confidence***. It assures us that what we are doing is the right thing. Jesus was the real-life example. The Gospel of Mathew tells a story in which Jesus healed a man who was blind and mute because he had a demon. When religious leaders saw that Jesus had the power to cast out demons, they accused Him of receiving His power from Beelzebul, the chief of demons. Jesus, unperturbed by their charges, used the image of a country or a family fighting within itself to show the falsehood of their allegations (Mathew 12:25-25, 27 – 28 GN).

Second, ***purpose provides protection.*** In some ways, this benefit is an extension of the first, because purpose gives the confidence that nothing can harm us until purpose is finished. Paul the Apostle had many instances that could have terminated his lie. But the man could not die before fulfilling purpose. Third ***purpose empowers perseverance.*** Fourth, ***purpose introduces and maintains objectivity.*** It permits a view of life that looks beyond the apparent surroundings and the obvious pitfalls. Lastly, ***purpose sustains contentment.*** It supports a tranquility that refuses to be ruffled by the changing circumstances and states that pass through our lives.

CHAPTER 11

Crafting a Clear Strategic Vision

The greatest gift ever given to mankind is not the gift of sight, but the gift of vision. Sight is a function of the eyes; vision is a function of the heart. Eyes that look are common, but eyes that see are rare. No invention, development, or great feat was even accomplished without the inspiring power of this mysterious source called vision.

Vision makes suffering and disappointment bearable. Vision generates hope in the midst of despair and provides endurance in tribulation. Vision inspires the depressed and motivates the discouraged. Without vision, life would be a study in cyclic frustration within a whirlwind of despair. Our world today is in desperate need of vision. *"Where there is no vision, the people perish: but he that keepeth the law, happy is he"*(**Proverbs 29:18**).

These words have been quoted and repeated by millions of people over the years. The full essence of his (Solomon) statement implies that where there is no revelation of the future, people perish. There are many who have no vision for their lives and wonder how to obtain one. There are others who have a vision, but are stuck in the mud of confusion not knowing what to do next

Then there are those who had a vision but have abandoned it because of discouragement, some measure of failure or frustration. If you are in one of these categories the Power of Vision is designed to help you understand the nature of Vision, define a vision, capture or recapture a personal vision, simplify your vision and document your vision.

Your vision is not ahead of you but it lies within you. Start seeing beyond eyes and live for the unseen. It is your vision that determines your destiny. *Dr. David Oyedepo in his Book "In pursuit of vision" he says Knowing that it is yours but not knowing how to get at it can be frustrating*. Isaiah 2:2-3 and Micah 4:1-2 makes it very clear that the unfolding of God's ways is what will bring down His glory upon the Church.

A discovery of vision and its pursuit is the gateway to the actualization of glorious destiny (Hagai 2:9). Isaac had a vision and was enviable among the Philistines (Gen 26:12-16). So, every child of God carries an enviable destiny. We are not to be pitied but envied. This means that vision deals with strategic leadership and you will be developed into a Strategic Leader and a Strategic Thinker.

Why people fail

People fail because of lack of vision as well as lack of knowledge (Prov 28:19; Hos 4:6). People fail because they don't know what they want to succeed in. In pursuit of your vision, you need not compare with anyone or feel jealousy towards anyone. People also fail because of lack of preparation to their assignment (Hab 2:2-3). Many people also fail due to lack of mentors which they need to follow or consult in case they are confronted with some issues of their vision.

Vision and Leadership

He who leads without a vision is simply walking. Leadership without vision is the abuse of human and resources. Leadership without vision is like the blind leading the blind. Vision gives power and where there is no vision power becomes destructive. Vision is not sight because sight is the function of the eyes. Vision is the function of the heart. Greatest enemy of your vision is your heart. We walk by faith and not by sight (1 Cor 4:18). Sight is limited to the capacity of your eyes as sight deals with what is, while vision embraces what could be.

Jeremiah 29:11 says, ***"I know the plans I have for you declares the Lord, plans to prosper you and not to harm you, plans to give you hope and a future."*** It is exciting to note that God has plans for us and He wants those plans to be fulfilled. Yet for this to happen we must follow His direction and guidance. Remember, it is His leading that makes someone a giant (Ps 23:1-4). An example is when Moses had died and Joshua was set to take over leadership of the Israelites to bring them into the Promised Land.

God said to Joshua, Moses is now dead but you have a big vision, it is your time now to fulfill your purpose (Joshua 1:7-8). In other words, God was saying you will be successful if you learn and follow my precepts and principles. The following 12 principles for fulfilling personal vision have been used by people of vision and are designed to protect, preserve and guarantee the fulfillment of your dream. If you can capture these principles, you will move beyond survival mode. You will become an overcomer and see your vision come to pass

Be directed by a clear vision

To fulfill your vision, you must have a clear guiding purpose for your life. Every successful leader in history has had one thing in common: They were directed by a clear vision: Moses, Joshua, David, Nehemiah are example of men of God that had clear vision. Abraham showed him the promised land and God said that is your vision (Gen 12:1-4).

Contribution to God's greater purpose can only be fulfilled if you know your personal vision (1 Cor 3:8-11). Clear guiding purpose will keep you from being distracted by nonessentials. Having clear guiding purpose will enable you to stay on track when you are tempted to be distracted by lesser or nonessential things.

You must choose where you want to go in life and then be decisive and faithful in carrying it out. Remember that the vision is not the same as a goal or ambition such as building a house or buying a car. Having a purpose and vision has to do with your life existence

Your true work is what you were born to do: Nehemiah 2:12 says, *"I had not told anyone what my God had put in my heart to do for Jerusalem."* The truth of the matter is that your vision will bother you until you act on it. When God gives you a vision and confirms it, nothing can stop it.

Your vision is a clear conception of something that is not yet reality, but which can exist. It is a strong image of a preferable future. This means that the present is not enough (Prov 4:18). Never settle for what you currently have. Vision is always a pushing envelop. It demands change by its very nature. Vision is always future – focused. Fulfill the action steps to fulfilling vision.

Know your potential for fulfilling vision

When you discover your dream, you will also discover your ability to fulfill it. You will never be successful in your vision until you truly understand your potential. Your potential is determined by the assignment God gave you to do. Whatever you were born to do, you are equipped to do (Phil 4:13). God gives ability to fulfill responsibility. When you discover your dream, you will also discover your ability.

God gave us the gift of imagination to keep us from focusing only on our present conditions. One thing that is clear in line with God's calling is His provision. He provides (Phil 4:19).God appoints, anoints, and distinguishes people. He does not like them to get lost in mediocrity and to reveal our true selves to the world. The ability to accomplish your vision is manifested when you say yes to your dream and obey God

Develop a concrete plan for your vision

To a man belong the plans of the heart (Proverbs 16:1). God makes the vision and we make the plans. The truth of the matter is when you discover your dream, you will also discover your ability to fulfill it. To be successful, you must have a clear plan. If you do not have a plan, God does not have anything specific to direct you in.

"To man belong the plans of the heart, but from the Lord comes the reply of the tongue" (Proverbs 16:1). God leaves the planning up to the heart of the person, but He will provide the explanation as to how the vision will be accomplished. *"In his heart a man plans his course, but the Lord determines his steps"* (Proverbs 16:9).

When a person receives an idea from God, it must be cultivated soon or the idea will go away. Many opportunities come to people, but they have no plan in place that would enable them to make something out of them. If you do not have a plan for your life, you have nothing to refer to when you want to make sure you are on track. A vision becomes a plan when it is captured, fleshed out, and written down. You cannot tell your plan to everyone because some people won't be able to handle it while you are making it.

CHAPTER 12

Diligence

The Bible has a lot to say about diligence. What is it? What should we be diligent about? And what does God promise for those who are diligent? Have you ever heard the admonition "You have got to be diligent!" Often parents, teachers, coworkers or bosses will remind, encourage or instruct others with those words. But what *is* diligence, and how are we to become diligent?

According to the *Oxford Universal Dictionary,* diligence is "careful attention, industry, assiduity; unremitting application, persistent endeavor." **One of the Greek words used for diligence is 'Spoude'. It means earnestness, zeal and business.** A diligent person is described as "assiduous, industrious, conscientious, thorough; not idle, not negligent, not lazy." The meaning of diligence in the Bible is the same, though as we will see, there is also a spiritual aspect to diligence.

Dr. David Oyedepo, author of the book 'Exploits in Ministry' defines diligence as simply hardwork. He says vision is not for the idle. Ministry is not for the lazy. Progress in life calls for a pressing. Every prize demands a press. Great success is recorded on diligent pursuit. He further points out that diligence involves investing your abilities, strength and all you have into the pursuit of your mission. Whatever God has called you to do, go about it diligently. Pursue your vision with all diligence. Success will not come to meet you in the house, you have to go looking for it (Oyedepo 2002).

In the same book Dr. David Oyedepo says. "Imagine a man who has been called into the work of the ministry, but who is still in his pajamas at 11 a.m., blowing some tongues! When he finally decides to leave the house, he goes pursuing people in their offices. After office hours, he targets some others in their homes. What is he looking for? Assistance, money, etc. He believes that the success of a ministry depends on the people one knows. This is a lie of the devil.

The success of a ministry lies in God who has called you and your diligence in the pursuit of that which He has committed into your hands. On the day I was commissioned into ministry, I made a statement, which I believe must have offended some people, judging from the reactions that followed. I narrated an encounter I had with God while praying. He had told me, "My son, you have two eyes. Can you make one to look up and the other to look down?" I tried it (I had never given it a thought before) and discovered it was not possible. He then said: "Whenever you are looking unto man, never claim you are looking unto Me; and whenever you are looking unto Me, you cannot be looking unto man.

But they that looked unto Me are lightened and their faces are not ashamed (Ps. 34:5). Look unto Me and you will not be ashamed. If you look unto men, you will fail." I am your source, I am your strength for the battle. I am all that you need, I am your sufficiency. The moment you start looking to any other source for help, you will fall woefully." He further says, when he rose up to speak, he declared emphatically, "God warned me not to rely on you."

*"By much slothfulness the building decayeth; and through idleness of the hands the house droppeth through." (***Ecclesiastes 10:18).**

Lazy and idle people never make any headway in life, because they are not operating God's formula for successful living diligence. Their closest companion becomes failure and defeat. Do you want to be successful? Then, be diligent.

*"Seest thou a man diligent in his business? he shall stand before kings; he shall not stand before mean men." (***Proverbs 22:29).**

Truly, God has said you will be the head and not the tail, you will be above only and not beneath (Deuteronomy 28:13). But the only way to get there is through a diligent pursuit of your goal. Only the diligent will rise to the top. The following is what Dr, David Oyedepo says in the same book, Exploits in Ministry: only the diligent will stand with kings. Our covenant fathers were not idle people. They were not lazy workers; they were hardworking and resourceful. When God called Abraham, He did not tell him to rear cattle.

Abraham could have relaxed and said, "I am called, so I do not need to work hard; I will still make it." He would have ended up a pauper. But Abraham laboured and God prospered him. God can only prosper the works of your hand, not your calling. He prospers your calling through prospering your efforts. Where do you think Isaac would have been if he had told himself, "God has told me to remain in the land of the Philistines and that He will bless me here, so I do not have to work. I will sit down and await His blessings"? He would have waited in vain. Maybe sudden death would have overtaken him, because of the harsh famine. But Isaac did not do this. Praise God!

The Bible records: "Isaac sowed in the land" The ground was tough, there was no rain in sight. His hands were sore and bleeding, the sun refused to cheer him up because it was harsh and scorching. But Isaac still sowed in the land. What happened next? The Bible says he received in the same year an hundredfold: and the Lord blessed him. And the man waxed great, and went forward, and grew until he became very great: For he had possession of flocks, and possession of herds, and great store of servants: and the Philistines envied him. Genesis 26:12-14 God prospered his hard work, not his begging or idleness.

There is no way you can impress God with idleness. Idleness is a carrier of poverty and it has no remedy. Invest in labour and reap the harvest. He that tilleth his land shall be satisfied with bread: but he that followeth vain persons is void of understanding. Proverbs 12:11 Backbiters are idle workers. It is only when you have no work to do that you sit down to talk about other people's shortcomings. Do you know it is only when you have stopped singing that you can know the person who misses his lines?

Learn to work hard and stop spending time backbiting. Hard work will take you to the forefront, where you will not be able to see people's backs. Laziness is a destroyer. It puts a man in a perpetual state of want, while the diligent never lacks. Hardwork is the pathway to progress. The more you apply yourself to hardwork, the better you become. Hardwork will take you to the top. A hard worker presses on in spite of all odds. Apostle Paul in one of his epistles stated:

"...How I kept back nothing that was profitable unto you"(Acts 20:20).

It was the same Paul that said: Know ye not that they which run in a race run all, but one receiveth the prize? So, run, that ye may obtain the prize. 1 Corinthians 9:24 He said run; not sit, think, wish, seek help, analyze. RUN! If you will not run, then you will not have the prize. The prize is for those that will run. Many have had visions of various magnitude and dimensions, but nothing has come out of them. The Word says you should write the vision and read, and as you read it, run to obtain; run to receive the prize, run to attain unto it.

Spectators or commentators take nothing home after a competition. Prizes do not belong to them, but to the active participants, "So run that ye may obtain." There is a time to write the vision, a time to read it, talk it, share it, and a time to run with the vision. The running phase is the winning phase! "So, run that ye may obtain." The running stage is like the planting and watering stages in farming. All the preparatory processes of the seed for planting can be likened to the writing, reading or sharing of vision.

But no matter how viable seeds are for planting, until they are actually planted and watered, no harvest is to be expected. If you expect a harvest, then plant like Paul and water like Apollo; that way, you have opened the way for God to bring the increases (1 Cor. 3:6). Yours is the task of planting and watering (running); God's business is to bring the increases. His task is to promote you. The emphasis is on the doing, not on the writing or the reading and sharing of the vision. It is the doing, the running.

In Paul's epistle to the Philippians, we see Paul's approach to ministry: Brethren, I count not myself to have apprehended: but this one thing I do, forgetting those things which are behind, and reaching forth unto those things which are before, I press toward the mark for the prize of the high calling of God in Christ Jesus. Let us therefore, as many as be perfect, be thus minded: and if in anything ye be otherwise minded, God shall reveal even this unto you. Philippians 3:13-15 A longing for more is the secret of Paul's success in ministry.

He was never satisfied! He looked forward perpetually, though without anxiety, to better days ahead and brighter results to come. Hear this

Apostle of renown: "I count not myself to have apprehended." No wonder he kept on pressing! If you get tired of the press, you won't receive the prize. This is why the Bible says: Woe to them that are at ease in Zion... Amos 6:1 everyone that will receive the prize requires an inner drive for an outward mark. It is time to challenge yourself towards landmark attainment. Press on, be diligent. If you will not run, and if you will not work, then you will not eat, neither will you be promoted.

For even when we were with you, this we commanded you, that if any would not work, neither should he eat. 2 Thessalonians 3:10. The basis for increase is output. Learn to work and invest your labour positively. God will surely reward the diligent. Those who press will surely obtain the prize. Those who run will definitely get the increase

What it takes to be diligent

There is a lot in the definition of diligence, yet to some people it all simply means hard work. Without a doubt, hard work is a part, but there is more we should understand. Notice an underlying thread is *responsibility and reliability*. People need to know they can rely on us to complete a given task to the absolute best of our ability. The diligent man or woman will make every effort to follow through on everything he or she starts, which requires self-discipline.

People with discipline have a goal, a vision of what is to be accomplished by their efforts. Keeping that vision in mind helps them stay focused and on task, even when the task at hand is laborious and tedious.

Diligence in the Bible

Solomon says in Ecclesiastes 9:10, **"Whatever your hand finds to do, do it with your might"** (that is, whatever you do, do it to the best of your ability). Jesus tells us, "Blessed is that servant whom his master, when he comes, will find so doing"—and not caught in idleness (Matthew 24:46). So, Jesus expects responsibility and conscientiousness from us.

He emphasizes this in Luke 16:12: "And if you have not been faithful in what is another man's, who will give you what is your own?" And, says

Jesus, "He who is faithful in what is least is faithful also in much; and he who is unjust in what is least is unjust also in much" (Luke 16:10). In other words, if you are not serious about small responsibilities, how will you be given greater ones? God regards diligence highly. We read in Proverbs 12:27: "Diligence is man's precious possession." Proverbs 21:5 amplifies: "The plans of the diligent lead surely to plenty."

In fact, God demands diligence! "You shall diligently keep the commandments of the LORD your God" (Deuteronomy 6:17). In Deuteronomy 28:1 we read, "If you diligently obey the voice of the LORD your God, ... the LORD your God will set you high above all nations of the earth." Hebrews 11:6 shows us how God takes diligence seriously: **"He is a rewarder of those who diligently seek Him."** God can see who is serious about seeking Him. We are to strive for the goals that He sets for us. We are to "seek first the kingdom of God and His righteousness" (Matthew 6:33), prizing these things above all else.

Joseph's example of diligence

As a young man, Joseph seemed to have all these qualities of diligence, and he provides us with a fascinating illustration to learn from. He had been sold into slavery by his jealous brothers (Genesis 37:28), and he was carried away to Egypt. There he was sold as a household slave to an officer named Potiphar (Genesis 39:1). But even as a slave, we see Joseph working with diligence.

We do not know much about his initial circumstances, but clearly whatever Potiphar gave him to do, Joseph very carefully and conscientiously did. In time Potiphar entrusted him with more responsibility, until Joseph was given responsibility for handling everything in the estate (verse 6). Diligence and God's blessings drastically changed his circumstances!

Will we be diligent?

How serious are we about the tasks in our life, including obedience to God? How diligent are we? Diligent people will expend tremendous effort to accomplish their goals. This is the attitude that God expects from us in everything.

This is the attitude we must demonstrate in the workplace, as Joseph did. Too many people want to put out minimum effort for maximum pay. But remember that Jesus tells us, "Just as you want men to do to you, you also do to them likewise" (Luke 6:31). Give your employers the same effort you would want from them if your positions were reversed. Finally, we see that tenacious diligence to the end leads to the ultimate prize. As Jesus promises in Revelation 2:10, We should strive now to be diligent in everything we do. The diligent person will find his or her home and family life improving, and diligent workers will often be rewarded on the job.

What does God expect of us?

Even more than in our physical endeavors, God expects us to be spiritually diligent. The old belief that God will accept you "as you are" is simply not true. God will not accept just anybody into His family—but only those who respond to His calling and choose to diligently follow Him. First, we must believe in the Lord Jesus Christ and accept Him as our Savior. That means we must sincerely repent of every sin and energetically seek God's help to change our lives—and that is not a simple or easy thing to do! We must diligently yield our lives to Him to use as He sees fit. Conversion involves an agreement between each individual and God. Ezekiel 36:27-28 explains: "I will put My Spirit within you and cause you to walk in My statutes, and you will keep My judgments and do them. Then ... you shall be My people, and I will be your God."

The diligent person's personal relationship with God grows and strengthens because of the effort he or she puts into learning from and obeying the Creator God. Finally, we see that tenacious diligence to the end leads to the ultimate prize. As Jesus promises in Revelation 2:10, "Be faithful until death, and I will give you the crown of life."

CHAPTER 13

Understanding Faith that Moves Mountains

Faith is a spiritual force that can move any mountain in a world of unlimited possibilities. Faith is the most potent force in the whole world and is a Key to achieving any desire in the kingdom. This is why there is need to understand the power that is imbedded in faith. Reader, you may wish to know that faith holds the key that opens impossible doors. When we observe in the scriptures Lazarus had been dead for four days, but when Jesus came on the scene He resurrected Lazarus from the grave, *"...And when he thus had spoken, he cried with a loud voice, Lazarus come forth"* (John 11:43).

Immediately that who was dead came out of the grave and came back to life. John 11:44 says, "And he that was dead came forth, bound hand and foot with grave clothes: and his face was bound about with a napkin". Jesus saith unto them,"loose him and let him go". Based on the above presentation, it shows that the enemy that the world has not yet found a solution for, is "death", but faith has a solution to it.

Faith is a Promise by God

Faith is one of the promises God made to man. What do I mean by that? All the promises of God are yours right now. Everything your heart could ever desire is contained in the promise within God's word. They already belong to you, but you have to receive them by faith.

Mark 11:23,*"For verily I say unto you, that whosoever shall say unto this mountain, Be thou removed and be thou cast into the sea; and shall not doubt in his heart, but shall believe that those things which he saith shall come to pass; he shall have whatsoever he saith"*.

This means that you will have what you say. This therefore is a call to avoid talking negative things about your life, your destiny, your career, your finances, your husband, your wife, your children, your relations, your business and even your dream. Remember that ***successful people tend to speak things they intend to see.*** While unsuccessful people tend to speak things they do not want to see. If you want to receive what belongs to you in Christ, begin to exercise the God kind of faith which I call faith that moves mountains.

Success in life comes from believing that God meant what He said in His word. Some people want to put their own interpretation on the Word of God. They want to read the Bible with denominational or theological glasses on. That should not be the case. There is nothing wrong with denominations or studying theology. But people get into trouble to understand the Word of God without depending on the Holy Spirit. When people read the Bible with eyes coloured by their own viewpoint, they can make the Bible say what they want it to say.

Faith Is All It Takes To Move Mountains

Every living aspect is faith generated. It is possible for one to become an enviable person through the God ordained assignment upon his or her life. Faith is what gets you there. It is important to usually engage faith with a view to tap into divine virtue, which in turn enhances your value. Your vision no matter how big it is can never deliver beyond the level of faith you are operating in. The beauty of success to every vision is a function of the quality of faith that is employed.

The colour of every destiny is a functionof one's quality of faith. Without faith your vision has no substance. Hebrews 11:1 says, ***"Now faith is the substance of things hoped for, the evidence of things not seen".*** Its faith that defines the substance of your vision. Every act of God in our lives is only realizable via faith. This means that as long as your faith is on fire, you remain unstoppable. Yes, you must know that it is according to your faith that mountains shall be moved.

Speak to Your Mountain

Let me start by asking you this important question. Have you ever looked at a mountain of impossibility and wondered what to do? God has provided a way for you to remove those hindrances and barriers that stand in the way of possessing all that God has for you in this life. God wants you to get every mountain of hindrance out of your way. You can possess your promised land which is the mountaintop of God's blessings in Christ.

"But upon mount Zion shall be deliverance, and there shall be holiness; and the house of Jacob shall possess their possessions". (Obadiah 17)

Your inheritance in Christ includes all the promises in God's Word. You do not have to wait until you get to Heaven to receive everything God has for you in this life. However, the question is "how do you receive all that belongs to you so you possess your own personal promised land? Your inheritance in Christ is exceedingly abundantly above all you can possibly ask or think.

Give Me This Mountain

At the time when the children of Israel were about to enter Canaan, the twelve Israelite spies went to spy out the Promised Land, only two of them were successful. Yes, even though all twelve saw the same things, the same giants and the same rich abundance of the land, Joshua and Caleb were the only ones who inherited their Promised Land.

The Anointing and Success of Caleb

Let us look at one of these spies, Caleb, to find out the secret of his success. Caleb went on to receive his promised land. Why was he able to possess the land he had seen forty years before? Caleb was a success in God because he totally dedicated himself to following God.

Numbers 32:11, 12

11 Surely none of the men that came out of Egypt, from twenty years old and upward, shall see the land which I sware unto Abraham, unto Isaac and unto Jacob: BECAUSE THEY HAVE NOT WHOLLY FOLLOWED ME:
12 Save CALEB the son of Jephunneh the Kenezite, and Joshua the son of Nun: for THEY HAVE WHOLLY FOLLOWED THE LORD.

To wholly follow the Lord means Caleb did not follow God halfheartedly. He did not follow God afar off. No, he totally followed God and every completely committed to do whatever God told him to do. Caleb followed God with every ounce of his being. And if God said stop he stopped. If God said go he started up again. He didnot question God; he just obeyed His instructions. This was the great key to Caleb success.

CHAPTER 14

Kingdom Fasting and Prayer Power

Prayer and fasting are the greatest weapons of war. Until you know the meaning of prayer and how to pray correctly, you will never be free from calamities. Prayer is not just communication, it is having the correct approach to communicating with God. Remember that the kingdom of God is a kingdom of Principles and everything must be done according to the guidelines of the Word, otherwise it will yield no results. *Unless prayer goes up nothing will come down.*

Prayer and fasting are the foundational base of every successful worshipper. Time spent with God is vital if you desire a fruitful Christian leaving. Results in life are achieved through prayer.Luke18:1 says, *"Men ought always to pray and not to faint."* Prayer is not an emotional release or an escape valve/ It is more than just asking God for favour. You should be getting results each time you pray. To get results from prayer you need to apply faith to your prayer.

Many people today just wish for results. Wishing is not the same as believing. Many failures are a result of not spending time together with God in prayer (poor fellowship with God). But from this day, make up your mind to be in fellowship with God. New birth will give you the right to expect your prayers to be answered.

"Now we know that God heareth not sinners: but if any man be a worshipper of God and doeth his will, him he heareth." Prayer is a sweet communion (fellowship with God). What a delightful experience.

People should engage in prayer and fasting more than anything else. This is why everyone in the kingdom must pray: The coloured; the Indians; Whites; Blacks must pray: Whether you are the victorious, successful, afflicted, the rich, the poor must pray.

The Force of Prayer and Fasting

Prayer and fasting are an effective force in the hand of a believer. The devil can be stopped and arrested by the force of prayer. Let God, arise his enemies be scattered: let them also that hate him flee before him (Ps. 68:1). As you read this book let your enemies be scattered in Jesus name. The three forces outlined for victory are faith, prayer and fasting. Do not sit down and wait for someone to pity you rise up, but engage the force of prayer to come out of your situation.

And when the devil had ended all the temptation he departed from Him for a season (Luke 4:13; LK 4:1-4; Math 4:1-4). The enemy kept coming back, but Jesus was always ready to defet him all the times: Beginning this day you will beat the devil in the face through prayer (Acts 16:25-31). If the devil has beaten you and kicked you to the floor it is time to rise up like a boxer in the ring. Listen, Champions are not those that never fall, but those when they had fallen, refused to remain on the floor. So, you need to stand up on your ground against the devil in prayer.

Prayer will provoke help from above. ***"Let us therefore come boldly unto the throne of grace, that we may obtain mercy, and find grace to help in time of need"*** **(Heb 4:16).**

Without help from above, we are helpless on earth. Prayer is not just telling God your needs, because He already knows them (LK6:32). It is getting Him to intervene in your situation on the basis of the word. Prayer aligns you into your desires. It processes help from above. The joy of prayer is that it brings mercy. "That we may obtain mercy, and find grace to help in time of need" (Hebrews 4:16).

David cried out for God's Mercy ***"Let us fall now in the hand of the Lord not the devil; for his mercies are great and let me not fall into the hand of man"*** (2 Sam 24:14). Prayer brings deliverance from Afflictions. Is any among you afflicted let him pray (James 5:13). Prayer Consecrates- it cleanses us from sins (1 Sam 11:14).

The Heart Preparation for Prayer and Fasting

There is no manifestation without preparation. Every encounter with God is born out of adequate preparations. 1 Sam 16:17 says, *"For the Lord seeth not as man seeth; for man looketh on the outward appearance, but the Lord looketh on the heart"* If the heart is not right, answers to prayers will not come. Prayers do not suit the wrong hearted. Prayer has its root in the heart and the heart is what matters most to God, Rom 10:10.

Preparing your heart in purity is the first step to establishing a viable communication with God, Sin is a barrier to prayers: Psalm 66:18 says, *"If I regard iniquity in my heart, the Lord will not hear me." You cannot embrace sin and expect God to embrace you.* As long as you remain in sin you are out of touch with God.

Your heart should also be prepared in respect to the word. Without the word every prayer ends in utter frustration. It is nothing but a worthless religious exercise. When you begin your prayer based on God's Word, you are starting with the answer. And this is the confidence that we have in him, that if we ask anything according to his will (the word of God), he heareth us (1 John 5:14). There is no point saying prayers that God does not hear.

Fasting a is prayer booster

You need covenant forces in prayer because there are certain oppositions that will not answer to faith and prayer alone. Such oppositions require you to build up stronger spiritual energy to deal with them. Fasting therefore is regarded as the prayer booster. Acts 13:2 says, *"As they ministered to the Lord, and fasted, the Holy Ghost said, separate me Barnabas and Saul for the work whereunto I have called them."*

The above scripture gives us a conclusion that prayer and fasting brings answers to human bogging questions. The separation of Paul and Barnabas was a function of prayer and fasting. Prayer and fasting will always bring results and answers to chronic challenges in life. *"Howbeit this kind goeth not out but by prayer and fasting."* (Mathew 17:21). The purpose of fasting is for the release of power (LK4:14). When we fast, we are not begging or struggling with the devil to leave but we are connecting with heaven to send the devil packing.

Hindrances to prayer

God wants to answer every prayer but they are hindrances to prayer. *"And all things, whatsoever ye shall ask in prayer, believing, ye shall receive."* (Mathew 21:22). This scripture means that we are to receive from God when we pray. But the reality on the ground shows that there are hindrances to prayer in some instances. Some of the hindrances include: doubt, unbelief, ignorance of the word, lack of knowledge of our right standing with God (James 5:16), unforgiveness and Strife.

*"And when ye stand praying, forgive if ye have fought against any: that your father also which is in heaven may forgive you your trespasses. But if you do forgive, neither will your Father which is in heaven forgive your trespasses."***(MK11:25-26).**

CHAPTER 15

Applying the Spirit of Wisdom and Revelation

kingdom of God is about the principle of Kings. The King who is God Himself is Key and central of the Kingdom of God. The Kings is preserved to be the ultimate source of authority and through His authority He established the kingdom. This means that the sovereignty of the king is reflected in his royal authority. The king of the Kingdom is never voted into power and cannot be voted out of power because the king's authority is by birth right. The king chooses who will be a citizen in his Kingdom.

"But you are a chosen generation, a royal priesthood, an holy nation, a peculiar people, that ye should shew forth the praises of him who hath called you out of darkness into his marvelous light"(1 Peter 2:9).

According to Genesis 1:1 the bible says "In the beginning God created the heavens and the earth." And Psalm 104:24 says, **"O LORD, how manifold are thy works! In wisdom hast thou made them all: the earth is full of thy riches"** Since creation, the wisdom of God has always visited the earth through human presentation. Each time these human vessels have operated by the wisdom of God, there is always a lifting and a rising glory.

The Nature of Wisdom and Revelation

Wisdom is the difference between failure and success. It is the difference between poverty and prosperity. It is the difference between sickness and healing, it is the difference between stagnation and fast progress. It is the best way to getting things done.

"Wisdom is the principal thing; therefore, get wisdom and with all thy getting get understanding"(Proverbs 4:7).

Based on the above scripture, wisdom can be also be defined as the correct application of scriptures to real life issues. Wisdom is about laying hold on the ways of God. It is not just mere mental exertion; it is discovering God's approach to every issue of life.

"That the God of our Lord Jesus Christ, the Father of glory, may give unto you the spirit of wisdom and revelation in the knowledge of him."(Ephesians 1:17).

Paul is revealing the importance of wisdom and revelation. Wisdom and revelation uncover how you can make the most of life and working it out at any time no matter who you are and where you are.

Principles of Wisdom

It is Creative

The word creation means to bring into existence. Nothing comes into existence through wishes but through implementation. Creativity activates reality. It is the power of bringing out something from nothing, just like God brought something glorious from nothing. *Theologians call this ex-nihilo, creation from nothing.* Wisdom is creative and it propels results in unexpected situations.

"Therefore, I say unto you, what things soever ye desire, when ye pray, believe that ye receive them and ye shall have them." (Mark 11:24)

It does not matter what you are passing through, using the word of God, you have the power to create your world. You can have what you say.

The forces of creativity are embedded in wisdom. We are called to join in the mystery of making things happen. This is what I call creativity and it can happen through the creative power of the word based on wisdom.

Self-Discovery

The discovery of self is perceived to be the greatest discovery in life. It is important that one should know who he or she is and understanding the reason for your existence. You need to know that you are unique, you are not a common person.

"And say to Archippus, Take heed to the ministry which thou hast received in the Lord, that thou fulfil it"(Colossians 4:17).

When God created man, He deposited a treasure in him. It is the explosion of that treasure that determines your position in society in general and in life in particular.

"A man's gift maketh room for him and bringeth him before great kings" (Proverbs 18:16).

What you think, what you do is a function of your gift. IT IS THE DISCOVERIES THAT MAKE PEOPLE DISCOVER YOU (EVERY SUCCESS IS ATTAINED AND SUSTAINED BY DISCOVERIES) (2 Tim 4:13; Daniel 9:2). Invest your time in the discovery of your gift.

Genesis 41:14, 15

*14 "Then Pharaoh sent and called Joseph and they brought him hastily out of the dungeoun and he shaved himself and changed his railment and came in unto Pharaoh" 15 "Pharaoh said unto Joseph I have dreamed a dream and there is none that can interpret it and I have heard say of thee that thou canst understand a dream to interpret it."*From this day your gift will take you to high places. The Gift will take you to Kings tables. Time has come and now is that time when people will hear of thee and that you have the answer to their problems.

It is a World of Dreamers

Once you are through reading this life changing book you will need to consider to join the dreamers' world. Why do I say so? We live in a world where only dreamers count. One of the ways on how God speaks is through dreams.

"In Gibeon the LORD appeared to Solomon in a dream by night: and God said, "Ask what I shall give thee" (1 Kings 3:5).

The scripture above is a function of revelation. After Solomon gave a sacrifice of over 1000 burnt offerings at Gibeon, God was moved and appeared to him in a dream and asked him what He should give him. In turn Solomon asked God to give him wisdom.

"And God gave Solomon wisdom and understanding exceeding much and largeness of heart, even as the sand that is on the sea shore." (1 Kings 4:29).

It is not enough to dream, you must also believe in your dreams. A dream is a mental picture of a desired end. Dreams are not night meres. A dream propels you to paint a picture of your desired end and supplies you with inner strength to fulfil it. So, to this end I say to you, dream! dream!dream!

CHAPTER 16

The Principle of Giving to the King

King and Kingdom are concepts that are of heavenly, not earthly origin. God chose these concepts to describe His plan and program for mankind and the earth. Thus, in order to understand God, we must understand the concept of Kingship and Kingdom. That has been the purpose and intent of this book. Adam was created as king and ruler of the earth. This is only natural. God created man in His own image and likeness, and because God was a King, man was to be a King as well. As King of the earth, man possessed certain unique qualities and characteristics that set him apart as distinct from all other creatures on the earth. One of these qualities was self-determination. Man possessed the ability to reason—to frame his own thoughts and ideas and to make his own decisions. In this he was like his Creator.

He was endowed also with the capacity for face-to-face, one-on-one intimate fellow-ship with God, a privilege that no other creature on earth enjoyed .The Creator gave Adam the earth as his domain because a King is not a king unless he has territory over which to rule. Through inappropriate use of his power of self-determination, Adam rebelled against God and lost his earthly kingdom. Man's rule over the earth was usurped by an "unemployed cherub," a rebellious and fallen angel who had no right or authority to take it.

Man became a slave in his own domain. But the gifts and calling of God are irrevocable (Rom. 11:29).God's original plan and purpose was still in place. Man's destiny was to rule the earth, so he had to get his kingdom back. When the time was right in history, the King of Heaven sent His Son to earth to reestablish Heaven's rule here. He sent His Son to restore man to his earthly kingdom. Jesus Christ entered the public eye proclaiming a simple but profound message: "Repent, for the kingdom of heaven is near" (Matt. 4:17b).

As a human as well as the Son of God, Jesus had the authority both to restore the kingdom and to rule it as King. Kingship was His birthright. Kingship is always a matter of birthright or genealogy. You will remember that when Jesus stood before Pilate, he asked Him if He was the king of the Jews, Jesus answered, "You are right in saying I am a king. In fact, for this reason was born..." (John 18:37b).

Jesus was not the only one to recognize His kingship. Even as early as His birth, there were those who knew who He was and why He had come: After Jesus was born in Bethlehem in Judea, during the time of King Herod, Magi from the east came to Jerusalem and asked, "Where is the one who has been born king of the Jews? We saw His star in the east and have come to worship Him" (Matthew 2:1-2).The coming of Jesus Christ as King demonstrates another important characteristic of God: He is a giver.

First, He gave man the earth to rule. Then, after man lost his kingdom, God gave His Son so that He could get man's kingdom back. Jesus gave Himself, even to the point of death, to salvage man from the effects and consequences of his rebellion against God. In the coming of Jesus, and throughout the Bible we see over and over that giving is a fundamental principle of the kingdom of God. God is a giver. In fact, His honor as King of Heaven demands a gift. As God, He gives because it is His nature. As kingdom citizens, we give because we are like Him, created in His image and likeness, and because giving is a proper way to honor a king.

The Royal Principles of giving

1.   The power of kings is displayed in their wealth

The wealthier the king, the greater his power (or at least the perception of his power in the eyes of others). This is why kings are always seeking to increase their wealth and expand their territory. The most obvious way that wealth displays a king's power is in his ability to give generously, lavishly, and even recklessly of his wealth to his citizens as well as to outsiders who visit his kingdom.

Kings who rule over lands that are sparse in resources and whose citizens are poor are judged to be poor kings, lacking in power and influence and therefore dismissed as unimportant. They may even be perceived as unable or unwilling to take proper care of their citizens and subjects. Poor kings, therefore, develop a poor reputation, which brings us to the second principle.

2. The purpose for a king's wealth is to secure his reputation—his glory

Every conscientious king wants to be known as good, benevolent, magnanimous, and just. He is constantly concerned for the complete welfare of his people. He wants to be able to show the world that he can provide his citizens with anything and everything they need. Want in a kingdom is a shame to the king. A king's reputation is tied to his ability to take care of his citizens, and that ability is directly related to his wealth. A king whose people are secure in his benevolent provision will be loved by his people, respected by other kings and rulers, and will enjoy a stable and secure reign. His reputation is firmly established, and his glory shines to all around.

3. The glory of a king is his power to out-give another king.

This is another reason why wealth is important to a King. Kings are deeply and continually concerned with the reputations and no king likes the thought that another King might be richer, more benevolent, or more giving than he. Consequently, kings will give freely in response to a gift given to them, or from pure beneficence, often wildly out of proportion to the value of the gift received or the merit of the recipient.

This is definitely a characteristic of the King of Heaven. As owner of literally everything, God is the richest King that was, is, or ever will be. No one can out-give God. And He gives lavishly with-out regard to our merit or our ability to repay. Do not forget that Jesus assured us that it was His Father's pleasure to give us the Kingdom. And He did not demand that we make ourselves "worthy" first.

4. Giving places a demand on the king's wealthy

Wealthy that is not used for anything serves no purpose. Righteous and benevolent kings do not seek riches simply for their own enrichment and pleasure. They do not acquire wealth just so they can sit atop the pile and say, "Look at me! See how rich I am!" Good kings use their wealth to bring prosperity to their people and improve the quality of their lives. This way the king's riches do not stagnate or rot away. In keeping with a fundamental principle of wealth-building, good kings know how to make their wealth work for them—they give it away in order to receive more.

It is a principle of reciprocity—giving begets giving. The principle of reciprocity works both ways. Giving to a king places a demand on his wealth because a king cannot allow himself to be out-given. Whatever he receives as a gift he must return in multiplied form. This brings us to the fifth principle of giving.

5.   Giving requires a response from the king.

When you give to a king, he is obligated not only to respond to your gift but also to exceed it.

When the queen of Sheba visited King Solomon, her gifts to him of spices, large quantities of gold and precious stones, was fitting proto-col. However, she was not prepared for the magnitude of wealth she found in Solomon's court: When the queen of Sheba saw all the wisdom of Solomon and the palace he had built, the food on his table, the seating of his officials, the attending servants in their robes, his cupbearers, and the burnt offerings he made at the temple of the Lord, she was overwhelmed.

She said to the King, "The report I heard in my own country about your achievements and your wisdom is true. But I did not believe these things until I came and saw with my own eyes. Indeed, not even half was told me; in wisdom and wealth you have far exceeded the report I heard. And she gave the king 120 talents of gold, large quantities of spices, and precious stones. Never again were so many spices brought in as those the queen of Sheba gave to King Solomon....King Solomon gave the queen of Sheba all she desired and asked for, besides what he had given her out of his royal bounty (1 Kings 10:4-7,10,13a, emphasis added). As lavish as the queen's gifts to Solomon were, his gifts to her in return far exceeded hers to him.

The King of Heaven is the same way. When we give to Him, He responds in kind but in much greater measure. Jesus said: Give, and it will be given to you. A good measure, pressed down, shaken together and running over, will be poured into your lap. For with the measure you use, it will be measured to you (Luke 6:38).We can never out-give God. Give, and He will give abundantly and overflowing in return. It is a principle of His kingdom. Besides, His reputation and glory are at stake.

6. Giving to a king attracts His wealth to the giver.

Giving begets giving. This principle works both ways. Kings give away wealth in order to gain more wealth. But when we give to the King, it begets giving back to us because our generosity attracts the King's wealth to us. This is directly related to the concept of stewardship versus ownership. As long as we feel we own what we have, we tend to cling to it and hold it close to our chest. In that posture, it is impossible to receive more. We cannot receive anything with closed fists and clenched fingers. On the other hand, when we approach the King open-handed with our things, not only can we lay them at His feet as a gift, but we are also in a posture to receive. Giving to the King attracts His wealth because He is a giver and is attracted to those who share a like spirit.

Reasons for giving to a King

1. Royal protocol requires that a gift must be presented when visiting a king

This is why the queen of Sheba brought such lavish gifts to King Solomon even though he was richer than she was. It was royal protocol. He would have done the same had he visited her. This protocol of presenting a gift to the king reflects a principle of heaven. When God gave Moses the Law for the nation of Israel. He made it clear that whenever the people came before the Lord, they were to bring an offering or a sacrifice of some kind, depending on the occasion.

They were never to approach Him with nothing. And even for the atonement of their sins on the day of atonement, God commanded Moses: And none shall appear before Me empty-handed (Exodus34:21b NKJV). Let us always approach the King with a gift of some kind to offer: a tithe or 10 percent of our income, praise, thanksgiving, worship; just not empty-handed. The best gift we can give Him is our heart and life, freely and completely.

2.   The gift must be fitting for the king

Worse than approaching a king with no gift is to bring a gift unworthy of him. An inappropriate or inadequate gift amount to an insult to the King. It shows that the giver does not properly respect the king or his authority. This is why the sacrificial laws of the Jews (which prefigure the sacrifice of Christ, the perfect Lamb of God who took away the sin of the world [see John 1:29]) stipulated that only spotless, unblemished, unflawed animals could be offered in sacrifice. The people were giving a gift to the King, and their gift had to be worthy of Him.

When King David of Israel set out to build an altar to the Lord, he sought to buy a threshing floor owned by a man named Araunah. Araunah graciously offered to give the threshing floor toDavid for his purposes:But the king replied to Araunah, "No, I insist on paying you for it. I will not sacrifice to the Lord my God burnt offerings that cost me nothing." David bought the threshing floor and the oxen and paid fifty shekels of silver for them" (2 Samuel 24:24).David was trying to stop a plague in the land caused by his own disobedience to God. After he built the altar and made sacrifices, God responded to his prayers and stopped the plague. Give a gift to the King that is worthy of Him. Do not offer some-thing that costs you nothing.

3.   The gift reveals our value or "worth-ship" of the King

The quality of what we offer the King and the attitude with which we offer it reveal much more than our words do of the value or worthiness we attach to Him. Quality does not mean a gift must be expensive or fancy, but it does mean offering our very best. And our gift does not necessarily have to be of monetary value. Of much greater value to the King is the gift of a heart that seeks first His Kingdom and His righteousness.

The Hebrew prophet Isaiah records the Lord's complaint against His people who devalue His "worthship": The Lord says: "These people come near to me with their mouth and honor me with their lips, but their hearts are far from me. Their worship of me is made up only of rules taught by men (Isaiah 29:13).Our gifts to the King should always be offered from a sincere heart and a humble recognition of His greatness and awe some majesty.

4. Worship demands a gift and giving is worship

"Worth-ship" is where we get "worship." To worship the King means to ascribe worth or worthiness to Him. And, as we have already seen, worship involves bringing Him a gift. There is no genuine worship without gift-giving. But giving is itself an act of worship, and worship is always fitting for the King. The Magi who saw His star in the east understood this, which is why they brought gifts when they came to find Him: On coming to the house, they saw the child with His mother Mary, and they bowed down and worshiped Him.

Then they opened their treasures and presented Him withgifts of gold and of incense and of myrhh (Matthew 2:11).Worship demands a gift, but it may be a gift of praise, a gift ofthanksgiving, a gift of confession, a gift of surrender, a gift of forgive-ness, or a gift of a tender and obedient heart as well as a monetarygift.

5. Giving to a king attracts his favor.

Kings are attracted to people who give with a willing and grateful spirit. Like anyone else, a king likes to know he is loved and appreciated. The King of Heaven is the same way. The Giver is attracted to the giver and extends His favor. Gifts open doors to blessings, opportunities, and prosperity: A gift opens the way for the giver and ushers him into the presence of the great (Proverbs 18:16).Those who know the protocol of giving gain access to the throne room, while those who do not, remain standing outside the gate. Giving from a generous heart with no thought or expectation of return particularly attracts the King's favor because that is the attitude closest to His own. And He rewards that kind of spirit: Anyone who receives a prophet because he is a prophet will receive a prophet's reward, and anyone who receives a righteous man because he is a righteous man will receive a righteous man's reward.

And if anyone gives even a cup of cold water to one of these little ones because he is My disciple, I tell you the truth, he will certainly not lose his reward (Matthew 10:41-42).To "receive" a prophet or a righteous man means to care for and supply that person with no expectation of repayment. Giving with no ulterior motive and with no strings attached—that is the kind of giving that attracts the favor of the King.

6. Giving to a king acknowledges his ownership of every-thing.

Remember, kings are also lords; they own every-thing in their domain. So, giving to a king is simply returning to him what is already his. That is why in the Kingdom of God, we are always stewards and never owners. This truth is embodied in the Bible in the principles of the first-fruits and the tithe.

Every harvest the Jews were required to bring the "firstfruits" of the harvest and offer them to the Lord. The same was to be done with all the firstborn of the animals: sheep, goats and cattle. In addition, a tithe—10 percent—of one's increase, one' sin come and produce, was to be given to the Lord. All of this was for the purpose of recognizing God's ownership— His Lordship—of everything and His benevolence and love in allowing them to use and prosper from His resources. These same principles apply today, at least in the spirit of acknowledging God's ownership. Kingdom citizens should still give the tithe regularly as an act of faith and of worship in recognizing not only God's ownership but also His daily provision of our needs as well as abundant blessings.

7. Giving to a King is thanksgiving

One of the best ways to express gratitude is with a gift. Gratitude expressed is in itself a gift. Look at the word "thanksgiving." Turn it around and you have, "giving thanks" or "giving gratitude." Everyone likes to know they are appreciated. Sometimes the best gift we can give a person is simply to express heartfelt thanks for a gift given or a kindness received. God is the same way. Expressing our thanks to God from a sincere heart for His blessings, kindness, and favor toward us is to offer Him a gift that He receives with delight.

Reasons why giving is natural for Kings

As Kingdom citizens and children of the King, we too are kings. That being the case, several principles follow:

1.   If we all are Kings, then we should give to each other.

Remember, you never approach a king without a gift.

2.   When we give to the Body, we give to Christ the King.

Because Christ lives in us through the Holy Spirit, every time we give to each other, we are giving to Him.

3.   Every time we meet one another, giving should be automatic

If we are to be like our King, who created us in His image and likeness, a giving spirit should be our nature.

4.   The wise men knew there was a greater King on earth

That is why they brought Him gifts and worshiped Him. He is still on earth—in the hearts and lives of His citizens. Whenever we give, we do so as if giving to Him.

5.   When you give to a King, you make a demand on what he possesses.

Giving begets giving. When we give to the King of Heaven, we obligate Him to give in return. This is not a presumptuous statement but the expression of a principle He established. When we give, He gives; when we withhold, He with holds. The ultimate and greatest gift the King wants from us is summed up in these words: Love the Lord your God with all your heart and with all your soul and with all your strength (Deuteronomy 6:5).Giving activates royal obligation. Give Him your life and receive His life.... remembering the words the Lord Jesus Himself said: "It is more blessed to give than to receive" (Acts 20:35)

Part IV

EXPLORING KINGDOM INVESTMENT OPPORTUNITIES

CHAPTER 17

Mastering Wealth Creation Principles

Life is a journey and it requires visions, expressions, intentions and ambitions to accomplish it. In this chapter you will learn the skills you will need to create wealth and be economically and financially empowered when you are in the Kingdom. It goes without saying that if you consistently do the things that other successful people do, nothing in the world can stop you from becoming a great success. This chapter is an attempt to provide practical tools and skills necessary to bring the vision for you. A vision is a description of the Road Map which answers three questions: Where are we: Where do we want to be and how do we get there.

The time we are living in calls for proper balance regarding the issue of financial and economic empowerment. Financial freedom demands that there must be a proper balance between these two extremes. Financial and Economic Empowerment simply means stewardship. It is the science of how one makes common sense decisions regarding money and other possessions. It also involves investing, allocating and controlling of resources. It is therefore the management of the resources of a household. It is the art of managing wealth. In other words, it is the art of building up and creating wealth.

It goes without saying that we all want to do better by staying wealthy, rich and abundant. And we are fascinated as well as envying those who already are. The question is how did they do it? What magic did they use? How can we do it too? The simple truth is that wealthy people tend to understand and do things the rest do not. The basis of the rules is that these are the things I have observed wealthy people do.

This means that if we do like them, we will become like them. This actually does work.

Wealth creation involves knowing what to do to make money, how to carry on making money, how to hang on it once you have got, how to spend, invest and enjoy money and make use of it altruistically. This assumes that you want to get richer, do it legally, do something useful with it once you have got it, put something back, keep some of this stuff under your hat and that you are prepared to put a bit of work. Therefore, this chapter is about thinking wealth, getting wealth, staying wealthy

Wealthy Creation involves establishing multiple sources of income that will fall on your income column producing net worth after expenses. In simple terms if you are in employment or business, if you do forward looking, how many days can you stay without your wage or salary?

And I will make of thee a great nation, and I will bless thee, and make thy name great; and thou shalt be a blessing (Genesis 12:2.).

Living a kingdom life has made me discover that the ultimate reason why God, the King of Kings and Lord of Lords would like to bless you is that He wants you to become wealth. The bible says that Abraham was rich in silver, gold and cattle (Genesis 13:2).

Wealth Thinking and the Kingdom

Money is a concept. You cannot really see or touch it. You can only do that with some physical symbol of it like bank notes or a cheque. Bits of paper yes but bits of paper with enormous power. When you live a kingdom life, money should not control you. The good news about becoming wealth and being economically and financially empowered is that anybody in the Kingdom can make money and that this is not selective or discriminatory. Proverbs 23:7 says, "As a man thinketh up in his heart so is he." This means that in the Kingdom we are products of what we think. In other words, you are the products of your thoughts.

Thoughts can make you wealth. Thoughts can make you move from one level to another level. This is a call to quality thinking and you will succeed living in the kingdom. Remember in the Kingdom you have the same rights and opportunities as everyone else to take as much as you want. Therefore, reorganize your thinking and begin to talk the things you want to see. God asked Jeremiah when His word came to him "What seest thou? And he said I see a rod of an almond tree." This is what I call the power of sight in the kingdom.

It also happened to Abraham. Genesis 13:14 and 15 says, "And the LORD said unto Abraham, after that Lot was separated from him, Lift up now thine eyes and look from the place where thou art northward, and southward, and eastward, and westward. For all the land which thou seest to thee will I give it, and to thy seed forever."

Financial Knowledge in the Kingdom

Knowledge is important and is power when living the kingdom life. *"My people are destroyed for lack of knowledge: because you have rejected knowledge, I will also reject you, that you shall be no priest to me: seeing thou hast forgotten the law of thy God, I will also forget thy children*(Hosea 4:6.Everything you know or believe about money did not come to you at birth.

You were conditioned in your attitude towards finances as you grew in your family or environment of your upbringing. Until the knowledge you have of finance is appropriate one for wealthy creation and Financial Empowerment, every plan you have gets messed up by the disjointed opinions you hold. Every time you want to create wealthy for economic empowerment, you might find at the back of your mind, things rising against it thus causing you make excuses and reject what finances are coming your way.

Thinking that money is scarce, evil, bad or dirty will make it hard for money to come to you until you get the right education. There are three forms of education: academic, professional and financial education. People are not wealth and even go to the extent of being poor because they are financially illiterate. They do not have financial education. To be financially mis educated is to use slow words like "I will never be rich or I will never become wealth". You must ask yourself how you will put your brain to work instead of asking how you can afford things.

Multiplying money is a skill and requires that you be adequately informed and continue to inform yourself on how to make money and see it increase. You must ask yourself how you will put your brain to work instead of asking how you can afford things. Wealth creation and financial empowerment rests in educating your mind and you need to know that being broke and being poor are not the same because if you are broke it is a temporary thing but poverty is eternal. You must educate yourself to know that multiplying money is necessary because money is a form of power and once you have it you have the ability to respond

How to become wealth and be financially empowered

Riches require that you have enough money. But wealth goes further. It is having enough of all the essential of life such as love, good healthy, friends and family, spiritually and of course, enough money. What we are saying is that being wealthy is a total package – laughter, love, living, good healthy, peace, money and relationships.

The following are proven ways on how you can become wealthy and financially empowered:

Wealthy and Financial Empowerment Thinking;

Developing an understanding of the power of small and big savings;

How to stay wealth and be financially empowered

Staying wealth in the kingdom requires that you spend less than you earn. Additionally, inculcate a culture of saving something out of each dollar and be responsible for where you are in life. Wealth people pay for purchases in cash and they use less credit. Living a wealth life also requires that you keep track of your money. This will help you not to lose money. Making money is like digging a hole while losing money is like pouring water in a pot full of holes

To maintain or sustain wealth as well as financial empowerment is a skill and it requires commitment to the proven wealthy principles. It is a matter of following the rules of the game. It goes without saying that those that love rules will be rulers and those that love commandments will be in command. To stay wealth requires you to follow certain rules. Here are the rules: don't spend it before you've got it:

- Put something aside for your old age – no more than that;
- Live a life of budgeting with a surplus focus. Put something aside for emergencies or rainy days – this the contingency fund; never

borrow money from friends or family but you can allow them to invest;

- Do not surrender equity;
- Know when to stop; never lend money to a friend unless you are prepared to write off;
- Find ways to give people money without them feeling they are in your debt and lastly share your wealthy.
- Sharing wealth simply means using wealth wisely.

"That they do good, that they be rich in good works ready to distribute willing to communicate"(1 Timothy 6:18).

Sharing wealth is the same as giving. We are not to be mere reservoirs that hold on to the blessing, but those who will pass it for others too to enjoy. When God called Abraham, He said He would bless him to be a blessing to his generation.

The process of giving and receiving is what makes the cycle of life to be perpetuated and be enjoyable.Those that keep to themselves do not increase.

There is that scatterth and yet increaseth and there is that with holdeth more than is meet but it tendereth to poverty.The liberal soul shall be made fat and that watereth shall be watered also himself" **(Proverbs 11:24-25)**

Chapter 18

Developing the Spirit of Industrialization

This book would not be complete without presenting or discussing the spirit of industrialization. Gone are the days when a pastor or leader of a local church should be sitting down and start writing letters to the friends and partners from well-off countries such as America, United Kingdom and Australia among others to ask for financial help. God has given us the wisdom and He is not a respecter of persons.

Acts 10:34, 35

34 "Then Peter opened his mouth, and said Of a truth I perceive that God is no respecter of persons." 35 But in every nation he that feareth him and worketh righteousness, is accepted with him."

The above scripture suggests that God can bless you in any location no matter who you are and where you are. Reader I ask you to lift up your eyes your blessing which you have been longing for all these years is just where you are. What follows are strategic entry into kingdom investments.

Start Up Business (Kingdom Investment) Opportunity

Starting a successful business however, requires preparation, special talents, skills, competencies and abilities, leadership skills as well as resources. These are critical requirements before you step into any business. Experience and observation has shown that many businesses both great and small fail because of poor or lack of preparation. You need to know that Prior Proper Preparation Prevents Poor Performance.

So I would like to say congratulations! The decision to start your own business can be one of the best you will ever make in your life. Owning your own business should be an exhilarating, inspiring, grand adventure; one full of new sights and experiences, delicious highs and occasional lows, tricky paths and, hopefully, big open sky's. But to ensure that your business journey will be a fruitful one, it is important to understand all that becoming an entrepreneur entails.

Setting up new business collides with the wishes of established competitors, who want all the customers' income they can get. Many people start their business adventure dreaming of riches and freedom. And while both are certainly possible, the first thing to understand is that there are tradeoffs when you decide to start a business. Difficult bosses, annoying coworkers, peculiar policies, demands upon your time, and limits on how much money you can make are traded for independence, creativity, opportunity, and power. But by the same token, you also swap a regular paycheck and benefits for no paycheck and no benefits. A life of security, comfort, and regularity is traded for one of uncertainty.

Start – up influences

Why does anybody want to take the risk of starting up their own business? It is hard work without guaranteed results. But millions do so every year around the world. The start-up is the bedrock of modern – day commercial wealth, the foundation of free-market economics upon which competition is based. So can economists shade light on the process?

Economists would tell us that new entrants into an industry can be expected when there is a rise in expected post-entry profitability for them. In other words, new entrants expect to make extra profits. Economists tell us that the rate of entry is related to the growth of the industry. They also tell us the entry is deterred by barriers such as high capital requirements, the existence of economies of scale, product differentiation and restricted access to necessary in puts and so on. What is more the rate of entry is lower in industries with high degrees of concentration where it may be assumed that firms combine to deter entry. However, research also tells us that whereas the rate of small firm start-up in these concentrated industries is lower, the rate of start-up for large firms is higher.

These seem useful, but perhaps obvious statements about start-ups, really happen and why? Somehow economists fail to explain convincingly the rationale for, and the process of, start-up. They seem to assume that there is a continuous flow of entrants into an industry just waiting for the possibility of extra profits. But people are not like that. They need to earn money to live; they have families who depend on them.

Benefits of Owning Own a Business or Company

Surveys show that owners of businesses or companies believe they work harder, earn more money and are happier than if they worked for someone or for a corporation. Before launching any business venture every potential entrepreneur should consider the benefits and opportunities of business ownership. The following are benefits of owning your own business:

- **Opportunity to Gain Control Over Your Own Destiny**

  One of the benefits of owning their own businesses that entrepreneurs cite is controlling their own destinies. Owning a business provides entrepreneurs the independence and opportunity to achieve what is important to them. Entrepreneurs want to "call the shots" in their lives and they use their businesses to bring this desire to life. They reap the intrinsic rewards of knowing they are the driving forces behind their businesses.

- **Opportunity to Reach Full Potential**

  Too many people find their work boring, unchallenging and unexciting. But to most entrepreneurs, there is little difference between work and play; and the two are synonymous. Roger Levin, founder of Levin Group, the largest dental practice management consulting firm in the world, says, "When I come to work every day, it's not a job for me. I am having fun!"

Entrepreneurs' businesses become the instrument for self – expression and self-actualization. Owning a business, challenges of all an entrepreneur's skills, abilities, creativity and determination. The only barrier to success are self-imposed.

- **Opportunity to Make a Difference**

  Increasingly, entrepreneurs are starting businesses because they see an opportunity to make a difference in a cause that is important to them.

- **Opportunity to Reap Unlimited Profits**

  Although money is not the primary force driving most entrepreneurs, the profits their businesses can earn are an important motivating factor in their decisions to launch business ventures. If accumulating wealth is high on your list of priorities, owning a business is usually the best way to achieve it. Research has shown that self-employed people are four times more likely to become millionaires than those who work for someone else.

- **Opportunity to Contribute to Society and be Recognized for Your Efforts**

  Often business owners are among the most respected and most trusted of their communities. Business deals based on trust and mutual respect are the hall mark of many established businesses owned by entrepreneurs. These entrepreneurs enjoy the trust and the recognition they receive from the customers whom they have served faithfully over the years.

- **Opportunity to Do What You Enjoy Doing**

  A common sentiment among entrepreneurs is that their work really isn't work. Most successful entrepreneurs choose to enter their particular business fields because they have an interest in them and enjoy those lines of work.

The following entry strategies have been presented to aspiring and existing entrepreneurs:

Finding Sponsorship

A safer bet as an entry wedge may be to take advantage of the willingness of someone to help sponsor the startup in some manner. Typically the sponsor is a customer, a supplier or an investor in the startup venture. A prime requisite for all these types of sponsorship is that the sponsor as credible and likely to succeed regard entrepreneur and the venture. The strongest basis for this is usually a track record of prior accomplishment and a demonstration that the entrepreneur possesses the capacity to perform the critical tasks of the venture.

Acquiring a Going Concern

Another strategy is to acquire a going concern. This can simplify the process of getting into business. A business can be viewed as basically a bundle of habits - customers buying, suppliers supplying, employees doing their jobs. In a going concern, those habits are already present. Expertise in a going concern should already be present in employees of the business. Even if it is not, the buying entrepreneur should be able to obtain education and operating help from the selling owner to fill in the expertise needed. Consequently, it is fairly common to find businesses owned by entrepreneurs who bought them with no prior experience in that particular line of business and nevertheless succeeded.

Developing a New Product or Service Opportunity

What it takes to start a company around a new product or service includes, most importantly, the discovery of an intersection between the market for that product or service and away to create one.

Creating Parallel Competition by Developing a New Product or Service

Parallel competition is often fierce. By definition it involves firms that lack strong differentiation and therefore tend to compete on price, which drives margins down. The toughness of such competition will likely force the entrepreneur to be good at performing the functions of the business.

Franchising Opportunities

One of the best ways to start a new business, if you do it right, is to buy a franchise or other established business. While people typically think of Mc- Donald's, KFC, Dunkin' Donuts, or Baskin Robbins when they think of franchises, the fact is that franchises come in almost every industry. The same is true for an already established business. They can be found for sale in every industry and take a lot of the risk out of the entrepreneurship equation.

Franchising is a method of distributing services or products. With a franchise system, the franchisor (the company selling the franchise) offers its trademark and business system to the buyer, or franchisee who pays a fee for the right to do business under the franchisor's name using the franchisor's methods. The franchisee is given instructions on how to run the business as the franchisor does using the franchisor's name and the franchisor supports the franchisee with expertise, training, advertising, and a proven system.

Buying into a proven system is important. The franchises that work best are those where the franchisor has worked out the kinks and translated its business into a systematic procedure that the franchisee follows. Do what the franchisor did, and you should get the results that it got; that's the idea. As franchisors are wont to say, when you buy a franchise, you are in business for yourself but not by yourself.

The reason that a franchise can be a smart business decision is that in right franchise system, the Franchisor has already made the mistakes so you don't have to. Franchising should reduce your risk. You need not reinvent the wheel. In exchange for its expertise, training, and help, however, you will be required to give up some independence and do things the franchisor's way.

Finding the Right Franchise

With so many franchise systems from which to choose, the options can be dizzying. It is best to start with a global perspective. In the universe of franchising, which industries seem to match your interests? Narrow the choices down to a few industries in which you are most interested, and then analyze your geographic area to see if there is a market for that type of business.

Once you have decided which industry interests you most and seems to have growth potential in your area, contact all the franchise companies in that field and ask them for information. Any reputable company will be happy to send you information at no cost. A great place to learn about all of your options is at a franchise trade show. This is a terrific way to gather a lot of preliminary information and survey the field in a short period of time, and you can find them in most good sized cities. When attending a franchise trade show, keep a few thoughts in mind. First, remember the companies exhibiting at the show by no means make up all of the franchise opportunities available. Indeed, these events showcase only a small selection of the available franchise programs.

Analyzing the Franchisor

As you go about this research, understand that successful franchisors have certain traits in common. Following are the traits that are most important. If you can find a franchisor that has these traits, you are headed in the right direction.

The Franchisor Supports the Franchisees

The best franchises are ones where the franchisor sees its relationship with the franchisees as a partnership. As Steve Reinemund, the former head of Pizza Hut, puts it, "Franchisees are only as successful as the parent company and the parent company is only as successful as the franchisees." Not only do such exceptional franchisors offer plenty of communication, opportunities for growth within the company, and help during hard times, they also offer lots of advice and training.

A good example of this is Dunkin' Donuts. To support new franchisees, it created Dunkin' Donuts University. There, franchisees and their personnel are invited to attend a six-week success program that teaches them everything from basic instructions on how to run the business to how to produce the products, deal with employees, and use equipment. It even offers advice on inventory control and accounting. Now that's support.

The Franchisor Is Committed To Customer Service

The great franchisors don't just give lip service to customer service, they teach it to everyone in the organization, and live it on a daily basis. That's critical, because if people are treated well at other outlets, that, in turn, gives your individual franchise a good name too. As the Pizza Hut chairman put it, "We are committed to more than just good service, we are committed to providing legendary service."

The Franchisor Changes with the Times

Tastes and values change. The last thing you want is to buy into a system that is stuck in the past, not realizing that its product or service needs to adapt to the times. The better franchise systems are constantly test marketing new ideas and new products in an effort to stay ahead of the competition. Typically, a good franchisor will provide the following services on an ongoing basis: Local, regional, and national advertising, offering you related programs and materials, field support, updates to the operating manual and ongoing related training for you and your management team. Some sort of advisory council, Research and development of new products, services, and system enhancements. Communication support—an intranet, a members-only Web site, monthly newsletters, or some other method to keep you up to date. If the franchisor you are considering does not offer these sorts of things, it would behoove you to think twice.

Location, Location, Location

Not all franchises need to pick a dynamite location. For example, janitorial services, direct mail companies, or lawn care services really don't need to worry about their location because drop-in business is not their business model. But a restaurant needs a good location. Typically, if you are looking at a retail establishment, location usually is a priority.

The first thing to do is speak with the potential franchisor. One of the best aspects of buying into a good franchise operation is that you should get plenty of advice and help from the franchisor. Start there and see what it says. The franchisor will know what you should look for, what works best, and what locations are available the franchisor will be helping you in the site selection process. Additionally, you need to find out about territorial exclusivity.

Does the franchisor offer this and, if so, what is the size of the territory? Territorial exclusivity has been the subject of many lawsuits between franchisees and franchisors, so make sure that you really understand this issue and have any agreements put in writing. As always, one of the best ways to know what to expect from a franchisor on this or any subject is to talk to the current franchisees. They will tell you if the franchisor plays fair, if territorial limits are respected, and if site location analysis is accurate.

Area Développment

A topic related to location is area development. Area development allows you to open more than one franchise in a certain locale. If, for example, you want to open and buy the rights to your area en masse. This allows you to monopolize the market and excludes challengers under the same franchise umbrella from competing with you. The key things to be considered in regard to area development are:-Picking a franchise system that is not yet developed in the area.Getting the franchisor to grant you market exclusivity.

Avoid Common Mistakes

Once all of your questions have been satisfactorily answered, you have done your due diligence and have spoken with existing franchisees, and you understand where your store will be located, it is time to sign on the dotted line. But before you do, make sure you avoid potential pitfalls. Franchisees often buy into a franchise without a full understanding of just what it takes to succeed in their chosen business. That is one of several common mistakes that are easily avoidable.

Buying an Existing Business

For many entrepreneurs the quickest way to enter a market is to purchase an existing business. Yet, the attraction of fast entry can a great mistake. Buying an existing business requires a great deal of analysis and evaluation to ensure that what you are really purchasing is really meats your needs. So you do not need to rush. For starters be sure that you have considered answers to the following questions:

- Is this the type of business you would like to operate?
- Do you know the negative aspects of this type of business?
- Is this the best market for this business?
- Do you know the critical factors for this business to be successful?
- Do you have experience required to run this type of business?
- Will you need to make any changes to the business?
- If the business is currently in a decline do you have what it takes to make it profitable?
- If the business is profitable why is the current owner want to sell it?
- Have you examined other businesses that are currently for sale?

Many of these questions ask you to be honest with yourself about your ability to operate the business successfully. On one hand buying an existing business has the following advantages: an established successful business may continue to be successful; the new owner can use the experience of the previous owner; the new owner hits the ground running; an existing business may already have the best location; employees and suppliers are already in place; equipment is installed and productive capacity is known and finding financing is easier.

On the other hand buying an existing business has the following disadvantages: It's a loser. A business may be for sale because it has never been profitable; the previous owner may have created ill will; current employees may not be suitable; the business location may become unnecessary; equipment and facilities may be obsolete; change and innovation may be difficult to implement; accounts receivable may be less than the face value and sometimes the business may be overpriced.

The Potential Drawbacks of Entrepreneurship

Although owning a business has many benefits and provide many opportunities anyone planning to enter the world of entrepreneurship should be aware of potential drawbacks.

- **Uncertainty of Income**

  Opening and running a business provides no guarantees that an entrepreneur will earn enough money to survive. Some businesses barely earn enough to provide the owner manager with an adequate income. In the early days of the business entrepreneurs often have trouble meeting financial obligations and may have to live on savings. The regularity of income that comes with working for someone is absent.

- **Risk of Losing Your Entire Invested Capital**

  The startup business failure rate often very high. Many studies have shown that 34 percent of new businesses fail within two years and 50 percent shut down within four years. Within six years, 60 percent of new businesses will have folded.

- **Long Hours and Hard Work**

Business startups often demand that owners keep nightmarish schedules. In many start – ups, 10 to 12 hour days and 6 or 7 day work – weeks with no paid vacations are the norm. Because they often must do everything themselves, owners experience intense, draining workdays.

- **Lower Quality of Life Until Business Gets Established**

The long hours and hard work needed to launch a company can take their toll on the remainder of an entrepreneur's life. Business owners often find that their roles as husband and wives or fathers and mothers take a back seat to their roles as company founders.

- **High Levels of Stress**

Launching and running a business can be extremely rewarding experience, but it also can be also a highly stressful one. Most entrepreneurs have made significant investments in their companies, have left behind the safety and security of a steady pay check and mortgaged everything they owned to get into business. Failure means total financial ruin as well as a serious psychological blow and that creates high levels of stress and anxiety.

- **Discouragement**

Launching a business requires much dedication, discipline and tenacity. A long the way to building a successful business, entrepreneurs will run headlong into many obstacles, some of which may appear to be insurmountable. Discouragement and disillusionment can set in but successful entrepreneurs know that every business encounters rough spots and that perseverance is required to get through them.

The Ten Deadly Mistakes of Entrepreneurship

Because of limited resources, inexperienced management and lack of financial stability, many business ventures suffer a mortality rate significantly higher than that of larger established businesses. Exploring the causes of business failure may help you avoid them.

- **Lack of Experience**

  An entrepreneur needs to have experience in the field he or she wants to enter. For example, if a person wants to open a retail clothing business, he should first work in a retail clothing store. This will give him practical experience as well as help him learn the nature of business. This type of experience can spell the difference between failure and success.
  Ideally, a prospective entrepreneur should have adequate technical ability; a working knowledge of the physical operations of the business; sufficient conceptual ability; the power to visualize, coordinate and integrate the various operations of the business into a synergistic whole and skill to manage people in the organization and motivate them to higher levels of performance.

- **Management Incompetence**

  In most business ventures management inexperience or poor decision making ability is the chief problem of the failing enterprise. The owner lacks leadership ability and knowledge necessary to make the business work.

- **Undercapitalization**

  Sound management is the key to entrepreneurial success and effective managers realize that any successful business venture requires proper financial control. The margin for error in managing finances is especially small for most entrepreneurs and neglecting to install proper financial controls is recipe for disaster. Two pitfalls affecting entrepreneurs' business financial health are common: undercapitalization and poor cash management.

Many entrepreneurs make the mistake of beginning their businesses on a "shoestring" which is a fatal error leading to business failure. Entrepreneurs tend to be overly optimistic and often underestimate the financial requirements of launching a business or the amount of time required for the business or company to become self – sustaining. As a result they start off undercapitalized and can never seem to catch up financially as their companies consume increasing amounts of cash to fuel growth.

- **Poor Cash Management**

Insufficient Cash Flow due to poor cash management is a common cause of business failure. Companies need adequate cash flow to thrive, without it a company is out of business. Maintaining adequate cash flow and to pay bills in a timely fashion is a constant challenge for most entrepreneurs especially those in a start – up phase or more established companies experiencing growth. Fast – growing companies devour cash fast! Poor credit and collection practices on accounts receivables, sloppy accounts payable practices that exert undue pressure on a company's cash balance and uncontrolled spending are common to many business ventures bankruptcies.

- **Lack of Strategic Management**

Too many entrepreneurs neglect the process of strategic management because they think that it is something that only benefits large companies. "I don't have the time" or "We are too small to develop a strategic plan," they often rationalize. Failure to plan usually results in failure to survive. Without a clear defined strategy a business has no sustainable basis for creating and maintaining a competitive edge in the market place.

- **Weak Market Effort**

Business success requires a sustained, creative marketing effort to draw a base of customers and to keep them coming back. Creative entrepreneurs find ways to market their businesses effectively to their target customers without breaking the bank.

- **Uncontrolled Growth**

Growth is a natural, healthy and desirable part of any business enterprise but it must be planned and controlled. Peter Drucker says that start – up companies can expect to outgrow their capital bases each time sales increase 40 to 50 percent. Ideally entrepreneurs finance the expansion of their companies by the profits they generate ("retained earnings") or by capital contributions from the owners, but most businesses wind up borrowing at least a portion of the capital investment.

- **Poor Location**

For any business choosing the right location and is partly an art and partly a science. Too often entrepreneurs select their locations without adequate research and investigation. Some beginning owners choose a particular location just because they noticed a vacant building. But the location principle is too critical to leave to chance. There is also need to consider the rate of rent. Location has two important features: what it costs and what it generates in the sales volume.

- **Inability to Make the "Entrepreneurial Transition"**

If a business fails, it is most likely to do so in its first five years of life. Making it over the "entrepreneurial start up hump," however, is no guarantee of business success. After the start up, growth usually requires a radically different style of leadership and management. Many businesses fail when their founders are unable to make the transition from entrepreneur to manager and are unwilling to bring professional management. The very abilities that make an entrepreneur successful often lead to managerial ineffectiveness. Growth requires entrepreneurs to delegate authority and to relinquish hands – on control to daily operations, something many entrepreneurs simply can't do. Their business's success requires that they avoid micromanaging and become preservers and promoters of their companies' vision, mission, core values and culture.

Putting Failure into Perspective

Because entrepreneurs are building businesses in an environment filled with uncertainty and shaped by rapid change, entrepreneurs recognize that failure is likely to be part of their lives they are not paralyzed by that fear. "The excitement of building a new business from scratch is far greater than the fear of failure." Says, one entrepreneur who failed several times before finally succeeding. Successful entrepreneurs have the attitude that failures are simply stepping stones along the path of success. This leads to a conclusion that failure is a natural part of the creative process. The only people who never fail are those who never do anything or never attempt anything new. One hall mark of successful entrepreneurs is to is the ability to fail intelligently, learning why they failed so that they can avoid making the same mistake again.

They know that business success does not depend on their ability to avoid making mistakes but to be open to the lessons each mistake brings. They learn from their failures and use them as fuel to push themselves closer to their ultimate target. Entrepreneurs are less worried about what about they might lose if they try something and fail than about what they miss if they fail to try. The entrepreneurial success requires both persistence and resilience, the ability to bounce back from failures.

How to Avoid the Pitfalls

As valuable as failure can be to the entrepreneurial process, no one sets out to fail. We have seen some of the most common reasons behind business failures. Now we must examine the ways to avoid becoming another failure statistic and gain insight into what makes a start – up successful. Entrepreneurial success requires much more than just a good idea for a product or service. It also takes solid plan execution, adequate resources such as capital and people, the ability to assemble and manage those resources and perseverance. Strategies to avoid the pitfalls include: knowing your business in depth; preparing a good business plan; managing financial resources well; understanding financial statements; managing people effectively; having a competitive advantage over rivals; leveraging (doing more with the less) and financial intelligence.

Part V

UNDERSTANDING TIMES AND SEASONS

CHAPTER 19

The Power of Understanding Times and Seasons

If you look to the horizon and see dark, billowing storm clouds forming, you know to grab your umbrella before leaving the house. If you are leaving for a vacation, the weather forecast allows you to look ahead so you know how to pack. You do not need much wisdom to read the signs. Even the Pharisees could read the signs of the weather, but Jesus considered them absolutely clueless in reading the obvious signs of the times (Matt 16:1-3).

But when we seek out the hidden signs, the Holy Spirit reveals to us what we should do and the best time to do it. The Bible talks about the children of Issachar. They had a rare attribute of understanding times and seasons. They also had an ability of knowing what to do in the marked times and seasons. **It** is no surprise that David wanted the sons of Issachar hanging around him. They were keenly aware of God's history with Israel and His promises for the future, which allowed them to perceive current and future conditions. They did not simply mark time. They correctly discerned time's effect to this present world, or changing seasons. As a result, they were able to craft appropriate and effective strategies.

They kept abreast of everything that was going on, but their minds were not easily changed by the popular belief of the day. I can imagine the sons of Issachar today watching a viral news story. They would not yield to the fear or anger of a super-charged story attempting to steal their focus. They would have noted patterns throughout recent history; identified the context surrounding the event; and most importantly, listened to God's promises and prophetic words about the event. I can hear them asking the Lord, "What do you have to say about this?"

I Chronicles 12:23 – 40 gives us a record of David's great army which was assembled at Hebron. We read of the thousands of warriors who came from every tribe. There were 6,800 from the tribe of Judah bearing shield and spear and from the tribe of Simeon, 7,100 mighty men of valor fit for war. The tribe of Zebulun is recorded to have 50,000 warriors who were expert in all weapons of war and who could keep ranks.

Amidst that list of thousands of mighty men, we read of the small number of chiefs from Issachar. Only 200 men, but they had an understanding of the times to know what Israel ought to do. These are the ones who carry the "strategy" within them that will defeat the enemy. Therefore, it is important that you and I understand the times that we are in. This calls for diligence in searching out the programme and timings of God, especially for our lives.

There are two sides of your life: the practical side and the prophetic side. The prophetic side of your life consists of those things that God has set in the place ahead of your coming into being but the practical side consists of those things that God will use to prepare you for the prophetic. How you interpret your current season determines whether you go to the next level of your life.

If Esther misinterpreted her time in Mordecai's house as a time of suffering and cheating, she would have missed out on the training meant for queens. For others, coming to midweek service may be a routine but for you it should be a major kingdom tool for preparing you for your divine destiny. Most talented people who ended up as failures misinterpreted their seasons.

Jesus asked his disciples "Will ye also go away?" and Peter said, "Lord, to whom shall we go? thou hast the words of eternal life." This means they considered it but they had no alternatives. No sane Christian should tell his wife "you are not the only woman in town" and expect a great marriage. Resolve it today; "my wife is the only woman for me" and do all that is necessary to build your home. God is the one that knows what He has prepared for you in destiny. He knows what to remove in you and what to add to you; He also chooses your training and trainer based on His purpose for your life.

Noble Bereans

The Apostle Paul found a synagogue of Jews in Berea and discovered they were a people who "received the word with all readiness, and searched the scriptures daily" to find out whether the Paul was telling them was the truth. Since the Bereans were open to the Word of God, they soon realized the truth of the gospel of Christ, and "many of them believed" (Acts 17:11-12).

James, the brother of Jesus exhorts us to **"receive with meekness the en-grafted (implanted) Word, which is able to save our souls"(James 1:22).**

So, to know the times and seasons is like the men of Issachar did, we must first search out the Word of God, discover the truth of the Word and allow it to be implanted deep within our heart.

Light Sets Time

In the first chapter of Genesis, the first book of the Bible, the story of creation is recorded. We are told that on the fourth day, God made the sun, moon and stars. They were created to give light to Day (the sun) and give light to Night (the moon). They were also created to "rule" – to govern or have dominion. Since Day and Night is a factor in Time, we see the LORD established light to set the times.

There are many scriptures which indicate the LORD has set timing, (Genesis 17:21; 21:2; Psalm 102:13; 119:126).

Since the beginning of creation, God has determined there would be times and seasons. Just as the natural man can observe a season change from summer to autumn, so the spiritual man can see and understand the change of seasons in the spiritual realm. By eating the Word and receiving the Holy Spirit, the spirit of man enlarges and becomes alert to the changing seasons. We too then, can have that same anointing as the children of Issachar.

Change the Times

Daniel knew that when "the time came for the saints to possess the Kingdom", the enemy, "shall persecute the saints of the Most High, and shall intend to make them miss set times by introducing contrary laws" (Daniel 7:25).Why does he do that? Satan knows if a set time is missed, then visions, dreams and supernatural conceptions will be aborted.

Time to Birth

When a Prophetic anointing is activated, revelation is received and "new things" are conceived. There are many ways revelation may come to a Believer in Christ. It may be through the written word of God. It may come in the form of a night dream or a day vision. It may come as a "Rhema" word when the Holy Spirit moves and speaks a word of knowledge to your spirit.

Birthing Anointing

The gift of prophecy cannot stand alone but needs the activation of the gift of giving (stewardship) to assist the birthing anointing. This giving gift is really the right provision provided at the set time. It can be spiritual giving through prayer and intercession, healing oil and the joy of new wine. It can be given in many natural ways with food, clothing and finances.

While most Prophets embrace risk, most Givers flee risk. Therefore, Givers often revert to a safe human agenda instead of giving the Prophet their last cruise of oil. If the enemy succeeds in making you miss your set time, the Prophetic will encounter the Ahab and Jezebel spirit. There are times when the Prophetic and the Giving anointing must embrace each other. The Prophet must be careful not to run ahead of God's set time, and the Giver must be concerned with supporting what our LORD has supernaturally conceived. Many who voluntarily give of their talents and resources will be surprised to discover they are "mid-wives" to new things God is creating on the earth.

While one may have a strong anointing in the Prophetic, another

Believer may have a larger Giver anointing. However, both the Prophetic and the Giver anointing can operate in an individual at the same time. We need to have our own individual God-given dreams but we also need to enlarge our tents to support other's visions. What season are you in? Is this the time to push through with the old visions and dreams that were birthed years ago? Or is this the time to be a midwife to someone else's newborn? As you look at the signposts around, the LORD may be asking you to do both.

The Advantage of Time Which You Did Not Know

Eternity is a timeless zone or realm. Eternity is one full day that never ends. If someone was to suffer in eternity for instance, how long will he suffer? It will be forever. If man lived in eternity, the circumstances we pray that will come to an end will never end. If the earth was designed to be like heaven – a timeless realm, then, there will be no end to evil and unpleasant circumstances, poverty, sorrow and sickness will never end. Nothing will change. Change is impossible in eternity. Anything in eternity stays on. Time is a temporary interruption in eternity. It is an instrument in measuring, assessing, planning and perfecting the inhabitants of the earth. In time, change is possible.

Anything you do not want, can be eliminated. In time, nothing is permanent – no condition is permanent. In time, a failure can become a success. In time, a child can become an adult. In time, the sick can become healed. In time, the imprisoned oppressed, afflicted can become delivered and reign in life. In time, what you cannot see in your today can be seen in your tomorrow. You can take advantage of time and seasons to change your circumstance and put in place what you long to see that is not in existence. Use time, do not waste it. Redeem the time and do not let it slip through your hands. Make most of every opportunity and do not let your God given opportunities slip through your hands.

"Making the most of every opportunity, because the days are evil". **(Ephesians 5:16).**

Opportunities are tied to the seasons of a man's life. Opportunities are created to move a man to the next season of his life. That is why you must understand the times and seasons of life. Become sensitive to identify and take advantage of opportunities that God creates to move you to your next level. The only time you have is NOW. Use it. Get busy and use it wisely.

19 Things You Must Know About Times and Seasons

1. God created time for measurement, assessment, planning and perfection

Time and seasons enable a man to measure and assess his growth, achievements, success, failures, and relationships, set goals and attain them. Change and excellence can be pursued and attained

2. The Life of every man is in phases and seasons

There is a time to be born, there is a time to die. There is a time to be young, there is a time to be old. There is a time to be a student, there is a time to be a graduate. There is a time to start a thing or project, and there is a time to finish it. There is time for sorrow and pain, there is a time for laughter and celebration. There is a time of lack and want, and there is a time of plenty and abundance. There is a time of failure and disappointment, and there is a time of success and accomplishment. There is a time of poverty and there is a time of prosperity. What experience you presently have can be changed if you will work hard at it. There is a time to be at the bottom, and there is a time to be at the top. God will move you to your next and better level in Jesus name.

3. There is a time for everything

Eccl 3:1-8 There is a time for everything, and a season for every activity under heaven. So, there is need learn how to use the right time for the right thing. Do not use the time for sowing for another thing, otherwise you will have nothing to harvest during the harvest season. Be at the right place at the right time. Always be on time. May God grant you the grace to be on time.

"For there is a proper time and procedure for every matter, though a man's misery weighs heavily upon him."(Eccl 8:6).

If he requires you to pray or attend a programme, before it will happen he will stir you up to do all that. If it requires your meeting someone, he will arrange a meeting. When it is time, the devil and circumstances that stopped you before, will no longer be able to stop you. When it is time, God will show up. And when he shows up, the devil will bow and situation will change. If God has not showed up, wait in faith for that is the purpose of understanding time and seasons. God will always show up in His time.

Today will soon become yesterday. The present will soon drift into the past. Therefore, you must redeem the time and make most of every opportunity. The future is pregnant with what you feed into it. You programme tomorrow with the values, habits, thoughts and deeds of yesterday and today. The decisions of today will determine and give results tomorrow. This is a call to make right decisions today. What you did not like yesterday, you can stop today. What you cannot see today, you can see tomorrow. It is just a matter of time. The beauty of time is that things change with time. To live in eternity the way we are now would have been horrible.

4. All you have is a season

When a man's season comes, things just go well. He labours little and reaps much; the enemy can no longer hinder or stop him. So, if things are going on too well for you and you are succeeding, I want you to know that all you have is a season. That you are in your season does not mean you know what to do. You need to wait on God to direct your path in order to flourish well in your season. When a man is in his season, things work out well not because he has the best strategy, works harder than others or prays more than others, it is his season. It will soon be your season. Wait for it. Many churches and ministries are succeeding because it is there season. Keep working hard in the vineyard as you are expected to by God, He will soon visit you when it is your time. Do not kill yourself or castigate others because things are not working so well for you. It is just a matter of time and your season will come.

6. Seasons pass, they donot last forever.

God created it that way to prove his supremacy, over all. It is time, all things change. Take a look at the churches for instance, one church rises to fame, and remains at the top for some years and suddenly another church or churches rise, and gradually, the fame and boom of that church begins to go down. The name of the new church or churches takes the center stage. All these are displays of times and seasons. As it is in churches, so it is in the life of individuals as far as their pursuit of purpose is concerned. We all have seasons, and seasons do pass. One man may be poor today, but rich tomorrow. One may be without honour today, but may be full of honour tomorrow. The difference between you and the other person is time and season.

6. Understanding time and season does not mean you should surrender to fate and not work hard

Laziness will only breed poverty but diligent hands bring wealth. (Prov. 10:4). Understanding of time and seasons gives peace, encourage patience, discourage and destroy envy and backbiting, but does not encourage laziness. You must continue to work very hard towards the pursuit of your life goals and assignment without looking back. Prov 14:23 23 All hard work brings a profit, but mere talk leads only to poverty. NIV Prov 28:19 19 He who works his land will have abundant food, but the one who chases fantasies will have his fill of poverty.

7. This world runs on a timetable

Though God prophesied the birth and ministry of Jesus in Genesis chapter 3 when the first couple sinned, God waited thousands of years before sending him. The devil and demons know that there is an appointed time for them to be locked up away from the earth. The devil knows there is a time to put him away. No matter how men raise a cry against the devil, he will not be put away until that time comes. Everything God has put in place in the world runs on a timetable.

8. You cannot bind on alter seasons

Winter must come when it is time for winter. The harvest season must come when it is time for harvest. It is a decree God has made and programmed. Nothing can change it. When it is your season to rise and shine, no one can stop you.

"As long as the earth endures, seedtime and harvest, cold and heat, summer and winter, day and night will never cease."(Gen 8:22 22)

No man's prayers or enchantments can stop a season from coming to pass. Summer must come when it is time.

9. Time solves all problems

God created time to solve all the problems that will crop up in a man's life. Every problem needs time to be solved. Patience is a necessary asset in reaping the benefits of time. No condition lasts forever. Never forget that.

10. Time is in the Hands of God

No one can delay the plan and purposes of God. If his promise has not come to pass, it simply means it is not time yet. He will show up at the appropriate time. His advice is that we wait for it because it is for an appointed time. Just as no one can delay the plan of God, no one can thwart the plan of God either. Time is in the hands of God. Your future is in the hands of God.

11. God's time is the best time

God knows what is best. For us and always does what is best. Anytime he shows up is the best time. All his plans and actions are based on justice and righteousness. There is no injustice or wickedness in God. Anytime he shows up is the best time, pursue your dream with zeal, work hard towards your expectations. Always believe he will show up now. If he does not show up now, keep believing. Any time he shows up is the best time. He has reasons for everything he does. He knows what you do not know, he sees what you do not see, he understands what you do not understand. It will be dangerous to give you what you are not matured to receive. God knows the changes that will take place in your life if your heart desire is granted now. So, he knows the right time to grant your request to create a positive change. God is never too early or late, he is always on time. God's time is the best time.

12. Time is money

Every minute used is money gained, and every minute lost is money lost. Time is to be used to gain money and fulfillment. Every training, profession, and business is for profit, profiting as in making money and being fulfilled. Time therefore is money. Every minute utilized will move you closer to your dream and goals in life. Do not be a time waster. Use time to your own advantage. Do not waste your time. Do not waste another person's time. Be time conscious. Be business like in your use of time. Always remember that time is money. Always go straight to the point and when you are through, excuse yourself out. Be mature in the use and management of time. Keep appointments. Be punctual, never keep anybody waiting. Build a reputation for being on time, and finishing on time. Time is money.

13. To waste time is to waste life

The days of man on earth are numbered. We haven't got forever to accomplish our God given assignments. We all have limited time; therefore, we cannot afford to waste it. A time wasted is a life wasted. You and I must aspire to die empty – totally fulfilled, having achieved all we were born to achieve. You must not die with what you were given by God to give this world. Always remember that time will never wait for you. You have to make every minute count. Use time and do not waste time. Time waits for nobody. It is either you use it or you lose it.

14. Time is not a commodity

Time cannot be sold or bought by anybody; Time can only be used or wasted. To regain time is an impossible task. It takes the supernatural power of God to gain back what one lost in time through the mercy and favour of God in a special package. Even then, there can never be another yesterday or a 100% repeat of any of the experience of the past. Once yesterday is past, you put it behind, and face today, while you look forward to tomorrow with hope. Do not deceive yourself, you can never buy or sell time.

15.   Time is one of the best gift God ever gave man

Understand it and use it to your advantage. Your financial worth, your relationship, your output will change for the better if you understand the value of time. Time is divided into three parts: Yesterday, Today and Tomorrow; Past, Present and future. What is in your past is past. Yesterday cannot be repeated but can oppress you if you let it. The past can help you to have a better future if you learn the lessons inherent in the past and use it for your own advantage. Today is the present. And what you make of today determines tomorrow.

Today will soon become yesterday. The present will soon drift into the past. Therefore, you must redeem the time and make most of every opportunity. The future is pregnant with what you feed into it. You programme tomorrow with the values, habits, thoughts and deeds of yesterday and today. The decisions of today will determine tomorrow. What you did not like yesterday you can stop today. What you cannot see today, you can see tomorrow. It is just a matter of time. The beauty of time is that things change with time. To live in eternity the way we are now would have been horrible.

CHAPTER 20

Managing through Challenging Times

Managing through challenging times can be a formidable task and a great key in life. *The word management in latin 'Manus' means office, handle or the art of getting things done. A knife cut be dangerous if it is not HANDLED properly in the kitchen. Even a burning pot can be so damaging if it is used without HANDLES. Management or Handling skills are what separates men from boys, women from girls. People can be in a similar challenging time, but some have the wisdom to extract chances from challenges, while others die off in challenging times.* I have also learnt that tough times are what separates managers from leaders and their followers. In this chapter I will share with you how to become a catalyst for change.

Before I proceed let me point out that when you are going through difficult times, your preparation for the future is as important as your performance in the present. Therefore, manage your challenging times to achieve your heroic aspirations. Questions such as "So what do I do or what should be done?" or surprisingly, there are no easy, or even particularly novel, answers to that question. But what comes clearly is that learning from what others have done before in the face of crisis can extremely be useful.

Ten proven and tested ways of how you can manage the challenging times.

1. Act quickly, but not reflexively and plan contingencies

It is worth to know that tough times are for immediate action. But even before you feel any pain, explicit contingency plans are a must. Keeping a pulse of emerging developments in your assignment will help you keep an eye out for potential roadblocks ahead. It is advisable to always plan for the worst, recognizing the troubles may unfold in fits and starts. Having plans B, C and in place and knowing when to move to each can mean the difference between pacing your life through a marathon and slippery slide.

2. Protect the core

While the bad news is that financial constraints may mean you cannot pursue all of your current activities, the good or at least the less bad news is that not all of them are equally important in terms of impact. Such times are the best times you need to allocate unrestricted funding and critical talent on areas that have greatest impact. It is also the time to consider whether you need to cut back or discontinue less critical activities and to ask yourself, "If not now, when?"

3. Identify the people who matter most and keep them strong

In life it is important to build successful relationships. You need to know that no man is an island. Your destiny is at the mercy of the relationship that you build. Relationship is essential for maximum results in whatever you are doing. Relationships in life are optional but obligatory for maximizing results

"Two are better than one, because they have a good reward for their labour" For if they fall the one will lift up his fellow: but woe to him that is alone when he falleth; for he hath not another to help him up" (Eccles 4:9-10).

There are three types of people that you will meet in life.

A. Destiny Suckers

These are type of people that leave you worse than they met you. They are exploiters and your remembrance of them is always with regrets. Beware of this kind. Examples of destiny suckers are;

friends of prodigal son and friends of Rehoboam, the son of King Solomon (Luke 15:1, Kings 12:18).

B. **Stagnation Agents (Those that leave you at the same level they found you)**

They do not add anything tangible to your life. There are certain people that you cannot trace any positive thing they added to your life.

C. **Destiny Helpers**

These leave you better than they met you and they add value to you. They will help you fulfill your vision easily. Every remembrance of them is full of rejoicing. Samuel and Saul, David and Jonathan, Barnabas and Saul are some examples.

4. Stay Very Close to Your helpers

The individuals such as your mentors and even organizations that know you best are the ones that are most likely to help you navigate a downturn. Remember that you do not have to wait for your key funders to call you. You should use this opportunity to call them: let them know what you are seeing and how you plan to respond. Explain to them the choices you are making or expect to make and ask them whether they can equally transparent with you in respect to any assistance.

5. Collaborate to reduce impact

This is the time to take some classic advice to heart: do not go through challenging times alone. Sometimes the most innovative solutions come from unexpected partners. Collaborations, of course require time and effort to make it work. Take care to weigh the likely costs, benefits and risks before proceeding.

6. **If it is an organization such as ministry or corporation involve your board**

It is in challenging times when your board must be well informed about the situation you are in. Board members can make important contributions in multiple ways: by providing experience and expertise from other domains and sectors; by helping to pressure test your assumptions and plans and by playing an active role in resource mobilization efforts among others. During the toughest times Board Members should be expected to be called upon. Effective work on their part, therefore, will likely require thoughtful and tactful management, not only on your part but also on that of your board chair.

7. **Communicate openly and often**

Managing your life or an organization whether it is ministry or corporation through tough times calls for open and frequent communication. People want to know what they can handle, where they stand, what your views are, and what they can do to help. Develop consistent talking points at all levels.

8. **Initiate Solutions**

In crisis situation you cannot wait to see what happens. You cannot leave things up to somebody else. Even if you are lying by the road side after a car accident and you cannot get up under your own power, the first thing you need to do is to pray and cry for help. You need to take some kind of initiative. If you have been injured you will have a long time of recovery ahead of you. Your whole life may be different. You need to initiate further solutions as you go along. You need to initiate solutions in order to get some control of an out – of control situation just as you would if you were in a war zone and needed to retake territory under enemy occupation.

David and Goliath in 1 Samuel 17 are a good example. The Philistine army had caused a military crisis by bringing the giant, Goliath to challenge the Israelites. Everybody was afraid of Goliath. Nobody thought they could win over such a formidable foe. But they had to, or they would be taken over by the Philistines. King Saul and his seasoned warriors were stalling for time. Along came David, who came to bring food to his brothers who were part of the army. He heard about Goliath challenge, and he knew that something had to be done. With a combination of God given courage and cleverness, David initiated a solution. He proposed that he himself a young shepherd, should confront the giant. The question that comes to mind is: "was this some kind of a joke?" How could a mere boy expect to succeed where well – armed warriors had failed?

9. Place Demands on Your Potential

There is need to take initiatives and place some demands on your potential. This means that your actions will somehow require you to draw on some gifts, some energy and some qualities such as courage that might have been hidden inside you. The truth is that you may never have gotten to use those things before. You may have to look for them. But your search will be rewarded, you may have more potential than you realize. To help you locate the gifts and character qualities that you are going to need, you must overcome a number of hindrances which I call them the enemies of your potential. These are disobedience, sin, fear, discouragement, procrastination, past failures, distractions, tradition, wrong environment, comparison, opposition and pressure from society.

10. Believe in Your Ability to Solve Problems

Whenever you are encountering challenges you must believe that you have the capacity to solve the problems you are facing. After all you are a child of the King and He can supply you with anything you may be lacking.

"Jesus said unto him, if thou canst believe, all things are possible to him that believeth" (Mark 9:23)

Your ability to solve problems in time of challenges stems from His unlimited ability to solve challenges. As a child of the King, your kingdom supply flows through your righteousness. Righteousness attracts God. He is righteous and He has made it possible for us to reflect His righteousness.

"But seek ye first the His kingdom and His righteousness, and all these things will be given to you as well" (Mathew 6:33).

The scripture above shows that if we fail to commit ourselves to a life of righteousness, we will never share in the riches of the kingdom. The riches of the kingdom include wisdom, discernment, blessings, wealth, power and understanding. Your ability to rise above a crisis and solve pressing challenges depends upon your maturity in Him. You know that this is true from your personal experience.

I hope the above ten tips on how you can manage your challenging times will be of help. You need to know that steps to manage through tough times tend to endure. Making the wrong choices ranging from across the board cuts that weaken everything you do, to fostering mistrust and fear by failing to communicate will have a long-term consequence. Make the right choices. It is one of the elements of success.

Conclusion

Let me conclude by saying, every nation and social civil society functions on laws and norms that make that society work. It is important to point out that these functions depend on the constitution and a body law that create a context and reference for social behavior and relating to the government and other members of the society. The result is a culture of laws and principles that serve as regulations, values, morals and standards that govern the citizen's relationship with the authority structure and its disposition as it relates to expectations within the constitutional framework.

In essence, all nations and Kingdoms contain inherent principles and laws that must be adhered to by each citizen in order for the citizen to benefit from his citizenship privileges and rights. These laws and principles are called by Jesus, "Keys of the Kingdom (Mathew 16:19). Failure to use Kingdom Keys in life is like having all information but not knowing how to use it, having all of this power available to us but not knowing how to apply it. Yes, it is like driving a vehicle a driving license. Therefore make a choice to start using Kingdom Keys today and watch how fast your success in life shall be.

Knowledge of the Word of God is important, but insufficient by itself for effective living as a believer. This is because most believers lack a proper Kingdom mind-set. Life in the kingdom is really about returning to the governing authority of God in the earth and learning how to live and function in that authority. Part of understanding the Kingdom is learning how to use the Keys of the kingdom. And this book just taught you how. Now go and use the Keys!!

References

"Barriers to Entry in Industrial Markets" Journal of Business and Industrial Marketing, Vol. 17 Issue 5 28. Lash, L.M. (1920),

Harvard Business Review Vol. 80 no. 11,pp99-105

Harvard Business Review <www.harvardbusinessonline.com Inc. www. inc.com Red Herring <www.redherring.com Wall Street Journal<www. wsj.com

Nellis, J. (2004), Essence of Business Economics (India: Prentice Hall Private Limited) 35. Nickles, W. McHugh, J. et al (2005), Understanding Business (New York: McGraw – Hill Class and growth" Business and Finance Review, pp 5 – 20 38. Own Your Own Corporation

Hagin, K.E., (1990) Prayer Secrets. Kenneth Hagin Ministries, Tulsa

Maxwell, J.C., (2007) How Successful People Think, Hachette Book Group, New York

Munroe, M., (2003) Principles of Power of Vision, Destiny Image, Nassau

Munroe, M., (2005) Kingdom Principles, Destiny Image, Nassau

Munroe, M., (2009) Overcoming Crisis, Destiny Image, Nassau

Munroe, M., (2005) Kingdom Principles,Destiny Image, Nassau

Munroe, M., (2012) Reclaiming Your Purpose, Destiny Image, Nassau

Business Venture, Harvard Business Review, July 26. Jones, G. (2005)

Murdoch, M., (2007) 2 Minute Wisdom, The Wisdom Centre, Denton Highway, TX

Oyedepo D., (2002) Exploits in Ministry, Dominion Publishing House, Logos

Oyedepo, D., (2012) Unlimited Power of Faith, Dominion Publishing House, Logos

Otabil, M., (2012) Seize Your Kailos Moment, International Central Gospel Church, Accra

Resnblun P. (2003), "Bottom Feeding for Blockbuster Business" Harvard Business Review Students, 2nd ed. (Great Britain: Ashford Colour Press Ltd)

Scarborough, M (2003), Effective Small Business, (USA: Pearson Education Limited) 51. 54. Stevenson, W. (2005), Operations Management, (New York: McGraw – Hill Companies, Inc) 55. Sullivan, D. (2001), International Business, (USA: Pearson Education Limited)

Volume 81 no. 3, pp52 – 59 49. Saunders, M. Lewis P. et al (2000), Research Methods of Business

Web Sites

www.business2.com

www.businessweek.com

www.entrepreneur.com

www.fastcompany.com

www.forbes.com

www.fortune.com

www.franchise1.com

www.aarpsmallbiz.com

www.asbdc-us.org

www.att.sbresources.com

www.bcentral.com

www.bizland.com

www.bloomberg.com

www.chamberbiz.com

www.entreworld.com

www.isquare.com

www.workz.com

Printed in the United States
by Baker & Taylor Publisher Services